Our Own Journeys

Readings for Cross-cultural Communication

Norine Dresser

LONGMAN ON THE **WEB**

Longman.com offers online resources for teachers and students. Access our Companion Websites, our online catalog, and our local offices around the world.

Visit us at **longman.com**.

Longman

Dedication

To the students attempting to learn English,
I salute you!
To the teachers who will discover
these pupils' folkways,
I envy you.

Our Own Journeys: Readings for Cross-cultural Communication

Copyright © 2003 by Pearson Education, Inc.
All rights reserved.
No part of this publication may be reproduced,
stored in a retrieval system, or transmitted
in any form or by any means, electronic, mechanical,
photocopying, recording, or otherwise,
without the prior permission of the publisher.

Pearson Education, 10 Bank Street, White Plains, NY 10606

Development director: Penny Laporte
Senior acquisitions editor: Laura Le Dréan
Development editor: Jane Sturtevant
Vice president, director of design and production: Rhea Banker
Executive managing editor: Linda Moser
Senior production manager: Ray Keating
Associate managing editor: Mike Kemper
Art director: Ann France
Senior manufacturing buyer: Dave Dickey
Cover design: Ann France
Text design: Proof Positive/Farrowlyne Associates, Inc.
Text composition: Proof Positive/Farrowlyne Associates, Inc.
Text font: 11/13 New Aster
Project management: Proof Positive/Farrowlyne Associates, Inc.
Text art: Kathie Kelleher/Portfolio Solutions, LLC; Andrew Shiff; Carol Stutz

Library of Congress Cataloging-in-Publication Data

Dresser, Norine.
    Our own journeys : readings for cross-cultural communication / Norine Dresser.
      p. cm.
    ISBN 0-13-048466-0 (pbk. : alk. paper)
    1. English language—Textbooks for foreign speakers. 2. Intercultural
communication—Problems, exercises, etc. 3. Readers—United States.
4. Readers—Culture. I. Title.

PE1128.D685 2003
428.6'4—dc21

                                                   2003047649

ISBN: 0-13-048466-0

Printed in the United States of America
1 2 3 4 5 6 7 8 9 10–VHG–08 07 06 05 04 03

✳ Contents

✸ Background

I have been a professional folklorist for over thirty years. I chose folklore for my life's work because folklorists study the ways and reasons humans celebrate, tell stories and jokes, sing, dance, play, cook, and eat. Fascination with folklore has led me to investigate a wide range of activities, including marriage customs in early California, cross-cultural birth, healing, and death rituals, ethnic food shopping habits, rumors, telephone pranks, even beliefs in vampires.

Our Own Journeys is an outgrowth of *Our Own Stories* (Longman, 1993, 1995). The original book evolved from stories told by my nonnative-English-speaking students at California State University, Los Angeles. They related their difficulties in understanding and being understood in the United States due to cultural differences. I became absorbed by the role of culture in miscommunication and wrote *I Felt Like I Was from Another Planet* (Addison-Wesley, 1994) as a guidebook for teachers dealing with students from diverse backgrounds enrolled in regular classrooms.

Another offshoot of *Our Own Stories* was a *Los Angeles Times* column, "Multicultural Manners" (1993–2001), and the book *Multicultural Manners* (Wiley, 1996). In 1998, these works received the John Anson Ford Award from the Los Angeles County Commission on Human Relations for demonstrating respect for diverse traditions. This recognition spurred me to continue collecting compelling tales of communication miscues caused by cultural differences.

Folklore provides a means of stimulating discussion. No matter if one converses with scholars, those struggling to learn English, or others, the content connects at an emotional level.

In sharing customs and beliefs with classmates, as *Our Own Journeys* encourages, students validate their own cultural backgrounds and simultaneously learn about their classmates' backgrounds. Thus, teachers can transform cultural differences into classroom assets. Students don't have to learn new information in order to communicate. They carry the data, their own folklore, within.

What better place to embrace diversity than in the ESL classroom? It is neutral ground, an ideal setting for talking about cultural differences. As a facilitator, the teacher can become a role model by showing respect for student differences. And when students feel valued and respected, learning happens. Teachers learn as well. We learn about our students, the world, and ourselves.

✳ Guide to Using the Book

Our Own Journeys is designed to help high-beginning-level English-language learners improve their conversation and reading skills and to supply information about the United States and other cultures. Each of the twenty units begins with a story of cultural differences causing miscommunication. The stories involve customs and beliefs from a variety of cultures and ethnicities.

Activities are self-explanatory. Although I sometimes recommend ways of working with the materials (pair work, group work), these are merely suggestions. I encourage teachers to adapt, amend, and expand on the activities in the book.

One of the great advantages of pair work is that, potentially, the student with better skills can become the teacher for the lesser-skilled student. Although as teachers we know that no student likes to appear less capable than another, nonetheless, if the teacher shows students how to ask a classmate for help, students will feel less vulnerable about doing it. If the better-skilled student feels confident, he or she will clarify the material for both parties, reinforcing his or her own understanding. Eventually, corrections from a peer will intimidate less than those from a teacher, and both students will benefit. Working in dyads and triads creates classroom energy. Working in small groups benefits shy students and reduces pressure on those worried about making mistakes.

Teachers may select a unit in or out of sequence, use it in one class meeting or extend it to another day. However, to get the most out of every unit, it is preferable to use all sections.

An answer key appears in the back of the book.

WHAT DO YOU THINK?

These questions introduce the topic of the story and the unit. The teacher may use the questions with the entire class to focus students' attention on the topic. Alternatively, students can answer the questions with partners.

The Story

These true stories are the heart of the unit. Every story sets up a situation where two cultures meet and a misunderstanding arises.

Students may read the story silently, the teacher may read it aloud to the students, or the students might read it aloud, each taking one sentence.

Every story mentions at least one geographic place—where the story happened or where one or more characters are from. There is a world map in the back of the book where these places are identified.

Can you guess?

Students try to guess the cause of the cultural misunderstanding. The purpose is to make students aware of their own assumptions about the characters' behavior and motivations. In some cases, this may bring out still more cultural misunderstandings, now on the students' part, rather than on the part of the characters.

Let's find out.

Here students discover the solution to the cultural puzzle. Finding out the real cause of the incident can often lead to introspection about students' own biases. For some, it may be an "Aha!" moment; for others, "I told you so!"

Later, teachers might ask students to choose a favorite part of the story or the explanation, read it aloud, and explain why it is meaningful to them personally. As a variation, students might create comic strips of their favorite stories. Returning to favorite past stories is also a good way to revisit and consolidate new understandings at the end of the school term.

COMPREHENSION

Two exercises follow each story. Section A focuses on details of the story to confirm knowledge of facts. Section B ensures that students grasp the main ideas. One or both parts of Comprehension can be used as a quiz. A quiz holds students accountable and gives them a feeling of accomplishment.

VOCABULARY

Vocabulary exercises are varied in order to maintain student interest. Students will get the most out of any exercise by first looking back at the story to find the words in context, then choosing the meaning for each word that the context suggests. The goal is for students to incorporate some of the words into their everyday lexicons.

✦ RETELL THE STORY

Retelling confirms that students have understood the story. Coming after Comprehension, which helps them understand important details, the sequence of events, and main ideas, and after Vocabulary, which can encourage them to try out new words, Part A gives students every chance to succeed in a well-defined oral task.

Not all students may be used to expressing their own opinions in class. Some may have difficulty in accepting that there is not necessarily a right or wrong answer to questions in this section. Part B of this section encourages students to voice their opinions and introduces them to the value of independent thinking. Students learn that it is acceptable to have a dissenting view. Many may find that having their opinions listened to is a new and empowering experience.

✦ DICTIONARY DISCOVERIES

Students need to learn how to use a dictionary. Most students are comfortable enough with bilingual dictionaries, but many are reluctant to use an English-only dictionary. Confidence comes with practice. Each time students open the dictionary to search for an answer, it becomes a less formidable task. When students complete all the exercises in all the units, they will have explored the dictionary more than eighty times.

These tasks show students the different things dictionaries can tell them and how to find what they need. Activities include alphabetic searching, finding information on parts of speech or pronunciation, and selecting the right definition based on the context. Example definitions come from the *Longman Basic Dictionary of American English* (1999), but tasks can be done with any English dictionary.

In eight units, the task involves finding the meaning of words in the story. In these units (2, 10, 12, 14, 16, 17, 19, and 20), Dictionary Discoveries follows Vocabulary rather than Retell the Story.

▲ CULTURE CAPSULE

Culture capsules describe specific aspects of culture in the United States related to the topic of the unit's story. A few questions follow to make sure that students have understood the essential information.

✦ CULTURAL EXCHANGE

After learning about U.S. customs or culture, students talk about their own backgrounds. Comparing cultures in this way stimulates lively discussion and helps students learn respect for one another's culture. As they talk, it is important that they avoid judgmental words like "strange" or "weird" or "superstition." Teachers might point out that one person's superstition may be another person's belief. They might also stress that it is important not to judge another culture without complete information about its values and customs.

Even if students share the same language and culture, or if they live in the United States and consider themselves Americans, they can gain from this section. Variations among families are interesting to discuss, and students can share any information they may happen to know about other cultures. Answering the questions in English will give them additional practice in listening and speaking skills.

EXPANSION

This section offers a wide variety of optional activities. Depending on need, teachers can assign them to students who finish other activities before the rest of the class, or use them for extra credit or homework.

OUR OWN STORIES

This speaking activity ties back to the opening story and gives closure to the unit. Students can give short oral presentations in pairs, in small groups, or to the entire class. After all the topic-driven activities, students should be confident enough to talk about themselves.

❋ Acknowledgments

First, I'd like to thank those who enthusiastically responded to my queries about cross-cultural customs: Navneet S. Arora; Katia Belooussova; Y. M. Chen, CMD., L.Ac.; Lanny Dryden; Carol and Isaac Haile Selassie. In addition, I am grateful to my faithful friends who listened to me ruminate and made insightful suggestions: Virginia Crane; Marilyn Elkins, Ph.D.; Montserrat Fontes; Clarice Gillis; Cheryl Rilly; Rachel Spector, Ph.D.; and Jan Steward.

I can't forget my family researchers either, volunteers and draftees alike. They were indispensable: Avi Berk, Zachary Berk, Carol Del Signore, Isa Del Signore Dresser, Amy Dresser, Andrea Dresser, Mark Dresser, Leila Sharafi, and especially Harold Dresser, househusband *extraordinaire*.

Finally, a unique "joint venture" best describes my association with the Longman Publishing Group. In 1991, when Joanne Dresner first phoned about doing the original *Our Own Stories*, I was recuperating from knee surgery. Later, in 2001, when Laura Le Dréan contacted me about writing *Our Own Journeys*, I was preparing for hip surgery. Then when I began working with Jane Sturtevant, my super Development Editor with whom I had instant rapport, I was recovering from shoulder surgery.

Unlike the surgeries, my relationship with Longman has been pleasurable and painless. Joanne, Laura, and Jane provided outstandingly professional and personable guidance throughout the process, for which I am most appreciative. I look forward to continuing my Longman connection but hope that I have run out of joints needing to be fixed.

UNIT 1
The New Year

WHAT DO YOU THINK?

➤ When do you celebrate the new year?

➤ Do some people celebrate the new year on a different date? Who? When?

Throwing Water

Read the story.

My name is Mrs. Buranen. I teach seventh grade in the United States. Usually my students behave very well—they almost never make trouble. But one April day some of my students were very excited and noisy. In the hall and on the playground, these students threw cups of water at each other. They even threw water at my teacher's aide and me!

I told the students to stop, but they continued their game. My teacher's aide didn't help me. She watched the students and smiled. Finally I got angry. I began to scold the noisy students, but my teacher's aide said, "Wait!"

Can you guess?

Work in a small group. Answer these questions.

► The students threw water. Their teacher told them to stop, but they didn't. Why not?

► Didn't they like their teacher?

► Can you think of any other explanation?

Let's find out.

Read the explanation.

The date was April 13. The teacher's aide told Mrs. Buranen that it was the Cambodian New Year. The aide knew this because she was from Cambodia. The students who threw the water were Cambodian, too. It is a Cambodian custom to throw water at others on New Year's Day. Cambodians believe that it brings good luck and happiness all year. Sometimes they color the water red, pink, or yellow to show their hopes for a happy future. The students threw water at Mrs. Buranen to wish her good luck for the new year.

Did the explanation surprise you? Why or why not?

◉ COMPREHENSION

A. Read the story and the explanation again. Write *T* (true) or *F* (false).

___T___ 1. Mrs. Buranen taught in the United States.

_____ 2. Cambodians begin the new year on January 1.

_____ 3. The Cambodian New Year is a serious and quiet time.

_____ 4. The students wanted to make trouble.

_____ 5. The teacher's aide was Cambodian.

_____ 6. The students wished to give Mrs. Buranen good luck.

B. Answer these questions in a small group.

1. Who did the students throw water at?

2. Why was Mrs. Buranen angry?

3. Why wasn't the teacher's aide angry?

4. Who understood the students?

◉ VOCABULARY

What do these words mean? Circle *a* or *b*. Look back at the story and the explanation if you need to.

1. behave well =

   a. be noisy and throw water

   (b.) be quiet and listen to the teacher

2. make trouble =

   a. behave well

   b. behave badly

3. a teacher's aide =

   a. a person who helps a teacher

   b. a teacher's book

4. finally =

   a. after everything

   b. before everything

5. scold =

    a. be angry at

    b. speak at in an angry way

6. good luck =

    a. when good things happen

    b. a lot of colored water

7. a custom =

    a. something you do any way you want

    b. something you do the special way your culture does it

RETELL THE STORY

A. Work with a partner. Student A, retell Mrs. Buranen's story. Student B, retell the explanation.

B. What do you think? Share your opinion with your partner.

1. Mrs. Buranen scolded the students. How did the students feel?
2. Mrs. Buranen's aide explained the custom to Mrs. Buranen. How did Mrs. Buranen feel?
3. The students threw water at their teacher. Were the students sorry?
4. In the future, will the students throw water at their teachers?

DICTIONARY DISCOVERIES

A dictionary is a book about words. You can find the meaning of a word, how to spell the word, and how to say it. The words in a dictionary are in ABC order. This is called *alphabetical order*.

The English Alphabet									
Aa	Bb	Cc	Dd	Ee	Ff	Gg	Hh	Ii	Jj
Kk	Ll	Mm	Nn	Oo	Pp	Qq	Rr	Ss	Tt
Uu	Vv	Ww	Xx	Yy	Zz				

A. Put these words in alphabetical order.

behave	aide	scold	celebrate	trouble	finally	luck

1. _aide_

2. _____

3. _____

4. _____

5. _____

6. _____

7. _trouble_

Put these words in alphabetical order.

seventh	student	stop	scold	show

8. _____

9. _____

10. _____

11. _____

12. _____

B. Choose three words from "Throwing Water." Find them in your dictionary. Write the word that comes before and after each of your words.

Example:

the word before   _scissors_

your word   _scold_

the word after   _scoop_

1. the word before   _____

   your word   _____

   the word after   _____

2. the word before   _____

   your word   _____

   the word after   _____

3. the word before   _____

   your word   _____

   the word after   _____

A. Read about New Year's Eve in the United States.

The year begins on January 1, but most Americans go to parties on New Year's Eve, December 31. At midnight, the new year begins. People make a lot of noise and kiss each other. It is a happy time. Many Americans also like to make New Year's resolutions. New Year's resolutions are promises people make to themselves to do something in the new year.

B. List three American customs you know about. Do you know other things Americans do on New Year's Eve or New Year's Day?

1. _____

_____

2. _____

_____

3. _____

_____

CULTURAL EXCHANGE

A. Ask and answer these questions with a partner.

1. Can you say "Happy New Year" in another language?

2. When does your family celebrate the new year?

3. How does your family celebrate? Do you eat special foods? Do you wear special clothing? What other New Year's customs do you have?

4. What do you do to bring good luck in the new year?

B. What do you know about other holidays around the world? Work in a group. Share what you know to complete the chart on page 7.

Holiday	Country	Date	Reason or Purpose	Activities
Girl's Day	Japan	March 3	Girls will think about being good and healthy.	Grandparents give their granddaughters special, traditional dolls.

✺ EXPANSION

A. How do most Americans celebrate the new year? How do you celebrate it? Do you do any of the same things?

Fill in the diagram. Then discuss it with a partner.

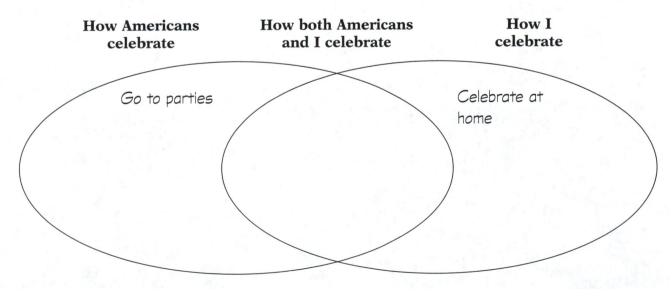

How Americans celebrate   **How both Americans and I celebrate**   **How I celebrate**

Go to parties

Celebrate at home

B. In the United States, many people make New Year's resolutions. Sometimes people promise themselves to lose weight, be kinder to others, study harder, or look for a better job.

Write three resolutions for yourself. Discuss them with a partner.

My New Year's Resolutions

Resolution	Reason
1.	1.
2.	2.
3.	3.

OUR OWN STORIES

Holidays are often the same every year. We see the same people and do the same things. Do you remember a holiday that was different one year? Tell your classmates about it. What was the holiday? Why was it different? How did you feel about it?

Luck

WHAT DO YOU THINK?

► Do you have good luck?

► Can a person keep bad luck away? How?

✹ Protecting the Baby

Read the story.

> One summer, I was traveling with my husband, Jon. We were on a crowded bus in Texas. Most of the passengers spoke Spanish. Suddenly, Jon said, "Natalie, look at those people with the beautiful baby." He pointed to a young family. They looked so happy. I smiled at them. Then, in my best Spanish, I said, *"¡Qué chulo!"* ("How charming!") and praised the baby.
>
> Now the parents did not look happy. They looked worried. They got up from their seats and came toward us. When they were close, the father held out the baby to me. He asked me to touch the baby.

Can you guess?

Work in a small group. Answer these questions.

► The parents looked worried. They wanted Natalie to touch the baby. Why?

► Did they think that Natalie wanted to hold the baby?

► Can you think of any other explanation?

Let's find out.

Read the explanation.

> The baby's father spoke to Natalie in Spanish. He said that praise from a stranger might bring bad luck. The baby could get sick or even die. But if Natalie touched the baby, Natalie was not a stranger anymore. Her praise could not hurt the baby. So the parents wanted Natalie to touch their baby—to protect him from bad luck. Natalie smiled and took the baby. She held him for a minute. The parents smiled too. Now their baby would not have bad luck.

Did the explanation surprise you? Why or why not?

COMPREHENSION

A. Read the story and the explanation again. Write the sentences in order.

Jon pointed to the couple and the baby.

The couple left their seats and went to Natalie.

Natalie smiled and said, *"¡Qué chulo!"*

~~Natalie held the baby.~~

~~Natalie and Jon got on the bus.~~

The father explained about strangers and bad luck.

The father asked Natalie to touch the baby.

Jon saw the couple with the baby.

1. Natalie and Jon got on the bus.

2. _____

3. _____

4. _____

5. _____

6. _____

7. _____

8. Natalie held the baby.

B. Answer these questions in a small group.

1. What did the parents believe about praise from strangers?

2. Did Natalie believe the same thing? How do you know?

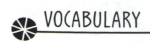

VOCABULARY

Rewrite the sentences. Use words from the box in place of the underlined words.

touch	pointed to	held the baby
worried	stranger	held out the baby
~~praised~~	protect	make bad things happen

1. Natalie <u>said something nice about</u> the baby.

   Natalie praised the baby.

2. Natalie was a <u>person who didn't know the baby</u>.

   _____

3. The parents were <u>afraid for their baby</u>.

   _____

4. Praise from a stranger could <u>bring bad luck</u> to the baby.

   _____

5. The father <u>gave the baby</u> to Natalie.

   _____

6. Natalie <u>took the baby in her arms</u>.

   _____

7. Jon <u>showed Natalie</u> the parents and the baby.

   _____

8. Natalie could <u>keep bad luck away from</u> the baby by holding him.

   _____

9. Natalie had to <u>put her hands on</u> the baby.

   _____

✸ DICTIONARY DISCOVERIES

Dictionaries give the meanings of words. The meanings are called *definitions*. If you want to know a definition, you *look up the word* in your dictionary. Here is the definition of *crowded*:

> **crowd·ed** /ˈkraʊdɪd/ *adjective*
> too full of people: *We had to wait in a crowded room.*

Look up these words in your dictionary. Write the definitions.

1. crowded   *too full of people* _____
2. passenger   _____
3. suddenly   _____
4. parent   _____
5. father   _____

✸ RETELL THE STORY

A. Work with a partner. Student A, retell Natalie's story. Student B, retell the explanation.

B. What do you think? Share your opinion with your partner.

1. The baby's father explained about strangers, praise, and bad luck. How did Natalie feel?

2. Can praise from strangers bring bad luck to babies? Can other things bring bad luck? What things?

3. In the story, did you like the baby's parents?

4. Did you like Natalie and Jon?

A. Read the information.

In the United States, some people believe that some actions bring bad luck. If you break a mirror, you will have bad luck. If you open an umbrella inside a house or walk under a ladder, you will have bad luck. If you talk about something that you want, you will not get it. If you accidentally talk about something that you want, you should "knock on wood"—you knock your hand on a desk or table or something else made of wood.

People think some things bring good luck. Sometimes people wear clothing that they believe brings good luck. Some people have lucky days or lucky numbers. Sometimes people see a falling star and think good luck is coming.

B. Work in a small group. Discuss these questions.

1. In the United States, what do people believe about good luck and bad luck?

2. What do you believe about good luck and bad luck?

CULTURAL EXCHANGE

Work in a group. Write the names of different places you know. What do people believe brings good luck and bad luck? Fill in the chart.

Name of Culture	Brings Good luck	Brings Bad Luck
1. the United States	you see a falling star	you walk under a ladder
2.		
3.		
4.		
5.		

EXPANSION

A. Draw a picture of something that brings good luck or that protects from bad luck. Write this information next to your picture.

1. What do you call it?

2. What do you do with it?

3. Does it bring good luck? Does it protect you? How?

Example:

This is a horseshoe. You hang it over the door of your house. It keeps good luck inside the house.

Discuss your picture with your classmates.

B. Take a survey.

1. Work with a group. Choose four things that many people think bring good or bad luck. Write them in column 1. (Everyone in your group should write the same things in column 1.)

2. Talk to five people outside of class. Fill in your chart. Write *yes* or *no*.

3. Work with your group again. Compare your charts. What did you find out?

Things That Bring Good or Bad Luck	Do They Believe It?				
	Person 1	Person 2	Person 3	Person 4	Person 5
1.					
2.					
3.					
4.					

OUR OWN STORIES

People believe different things about good luck and bad luck. Did anyone ever believe something that surprised you? Tell your classmates about it. Who was the person? What did he or she believe?

UNIT 3
Gestures

WHAT DO YOU THINK?

► Do you ever say yes or no without using words? How?

► Do you ever use any other gestures, or actions, in place of words? What are the gestures? What do they mean?

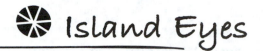 Island Eyes

Read the story.

> My name is Nick. I'm from Canada. In 1998, I was on the island of Pohnpei in the Pacific Ocean. I went to teach at a school there. On my first day on the island, something unusual happened.
>
> It was very hot, and I was thirsty. I went into a small store. I spoke to the woman behind the counter. "Do you have any cold drinks?" I asked.
>
> The woman looked at me, but she didn't say anything. I thought she didn't understand me, so I tried easier words. "Do you have Coke?"
>
> Again, the woman was silent. She didn't answer, so I thought that she didn't have any Coke. I spoke louder and more slowly. "Do you have anything else?"
>
> The woman walked over to a refrigerator. She opened the door and pointed to many different kinds of soda. She didn't say anything, but she removed a Coke and put it on the counter. Speaking slowly and clearly, I asked, "How much does it cost?"
>
> In perfect English, she answered, "Fifty cents."

Can you guess?

Work in a small group. Answer these questions.

► Nick asked three questions and the woman didn't say anything. Why didn't the woman answer?

► Nick was a stranger. Is that the reason?

► Can you think of any other explanation?

Let's find out.

Read the explanation.

> On Pohnpei, people say yes by raising their eyebrows a little. The woman raised her eyebrows when Nick asked questions. Nick did not see her gesture because it had no meaning for him. In Canada, raised eyebrows do not answer questions. Canadian people speak or move their heads up and down to say yes.
>
> Later, Nick found out that all of the people on Pohnpei raise their eyebrows to say yes.

Did the explanation surprise you? Why or why not?

COMPREHENSION

A. Read the story and the explanation again. Write _T_ (true) or _F_ (false).

_F_ 1. In 1998, Nick went to Canada.

____ 2. Pohnpei is an island in the Atlantic Ocean.

____ 3. Nick was a teacher.

____ 4. Nick wanted to buy a cold drink.

____ 5. The woman did not have any Coke.

____ 6. The woman did not understand Nick.

____ 7. Nick did not understand the woman.

B. Answer these questions in a small group.

1. How do people say yes on Pohnpei? Did Nick know this?

2. How do people say yes in Canada? Did the woman in the store know this?

3. What finally happened?

VOCABULARY

What do the underlined words mean? Circle _a_ or _b_.

1. Something <u>unusual</u> happened.

   a. the same

   (b.) different

2. I <u>was thirsty</u>.

   a. wanted something to eat

   b. wanted something to drink

3. The woman <u>was silent</u>.

   a. didn't speak

   b. spoke a lot

4. She <u>removed</u> a Coke.

   a. pointed to

   b. took out

5. She put a Coke on the <u>counter</u>.

    a. something like a table or desk in a store

    b. a machine for counting money in a store

6. The woman answered in <u>perfect</u> English.

    a. correct

    b. incorrect

7. Nick did not see the <u>gesture</u>.

    a. movement that has meaning

    b. cold drink

8. Nick <u>found out</u> about raised eyebrows.

    a. learned

    b. forgot

RETELL THE STORY

A. **Work with a partner. Student A, retell Nick's story. Student B, retell the explanation.**

B. **What do you think? Share your opinion with your partner.**

1. What did the woman think about Nick?

2. Imagine you are in Nick's situation (living on Pohnpei). Do you raise your eyebrows to say yes?

3. Imagine you move to another country. Should you change your gestures?

Guide words can help you find words quickly. There are guide words at the top of every dictionary page. Guide words show the first word on the left page and the last word on the right page.

These pages include words that come between *reform* and *rely* in alphabetical order.

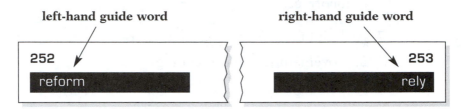

In alphabetical order, *refrigerator* comes after *reform* and before *rely*. So *refrigerator* is on these pages in this dictionary. Look up *refrigerator* in your dictionary. What are the guide words?

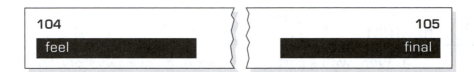

Is *fifty* on these pages? The answer is yes. In alphabetical order, *fifty* comes after *feel* and before *final*.

Is *face* on these pages? The answer is no. In alphabetical order, *face* comes before *feel*.

Is *find out* on these pages? The answer is no. In alphabetical order, *find out* comes after *final*.

Look at the guide words in each item. Then answer the questions with *yes* or *no*. Discuss your answers with a partner.

1. concerned / consume   Is *counter* on these pages?   _no_

2. single / slant   Is *slowly* on these pages?   _____

3. explore / eyesight   Is *eyebrow* on these pages?   _____

4. telephone / Thanksgiving   Is *thirsty* on these pages?   _____

5. escalator / exceptionally   Is *everyone* on these pages?   _____

A. Here are some common gestures in the United States. Look at the gestures and their meanings.

Yes.	**No.**	**I don't know.**
I hope so.	**Come here.**	**Goodbye.**

B. Do any of the gestures have different meanings for you? Discuss your answers in a small group.

CULTURAL EXCHANGE

A. Discuss these questions with your classmates.

1. A smile can mean different things in different cultures. What does a smile mean to you?

2. A *wink* is closing one eye and quickly opening it. A wink can mean different things in different cultures. What does a wink mean to you?

B. Work with a partner. Do you use gestures for these meanings? Show your partner.

Yes.	Hello.	Come here.	I don't know.
No.	Goodbye.	Stop!	Go away.

A. Play a game with two teams. One person makes a gesture. The other team tries to guess the meaning. Use the gestures in the Culture Capsule or other gestures that you know.

B. Draw a picture of a gesture that you use. Write answers to these questions.

1. What does the gesture mean?

2. When do you use it?

3. Who do you use it with? Friends? Family?

Example:

She is sending someone a kiss.

You do this when you say goodbye.

You do this with family members or very close friends.

OUR OWN STORIES

Tell your classmates about a time when you used a gesture to say something important. Who did you make the gesture to? What gesture did you use? Why was it important?

UNIT 4

Table Manners

WHAT DO YOU THINK?

► Are table manners important?

► Did anyone ever correct your table manners?

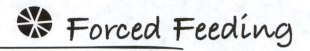

Forced Feeding

Read the story.

> My name is Eskinder. I was born in Ethiopia, but now I live in the United States. My wife is American. Her name is Lucy. My best friend is Isaac. He recently moved here from Ethiopia. One day, he invited us to eat Ethiopian food in his home.
>
> Lucy wasn't worried. She knew many Ethiopian eating customs. She knew how to eat with her fingers. She knew how to use our bread. We call it *injera*. We use it like a spoon to scoop up food.
>
> That night Isaac made Ethiopian stew. At the table, Isaac took a piece of *injera*. He scooped up some stew with the *injera*. Then Isaac held out the food and put it into Lucy's mouth. Lucy was surprised. She didn't know what to do.

Can you guess?

Work in a small group. Answer these questions.

► Isaac took some food. Then he put the food into Lucy's mouth. Why?

► Did Lucy need help?

► Can you think of any other explanation?

Let's find out.

Read the explanation.

> In Ethiopia, to start a meal, the host takes some food and holds the food up to the guest's mouth. The guest eats this food from the host's hand. Lucy did not know this Ethiopian eating custom. Isaac was making Lucy an honored guest, but she did not understand.
>
> Americans do not eat food from someone else's hand. Isaac did not know this. He did not know that Lucy would be surprised.

Did the explanation surprise you? Why or why not?

COMPREHENSION

A. Read the story and the explanation again. Write _T_ (true) or _F_ (false).

   _F_   1. Lucy is Eskinder's best friend.

   _____   2. Isaac came to the United States a short time ago.

   _____   3. Lucy was worried about Ethiopian eating customs.

   _____   4. Lucy and Eskinder went to Isaac's home for dinner.

   _____   5. Ethiopian stew is called _injera_.

   _____   6. Ethiopians usually eat with spoons.

   _____   7. Isaac ate all of Lucy's food.

   _____   8. Lucy didn't know all of Ethiopia's eating customs.

   _____   9. Isaac didn't know that Lucy would be surprised.

B. Answer these questions in a small group.

1. Isaac took some food. Then he put it into Lucy's mouth. Why?
2. Why was Lucy surprised?

VOCABULARY

Look at the story and the explanation. Match the words in _A_ with the meanings in _B_.

	A		B
_d_	1. invite		a. a person who goes to the party
____	2. fingers		b. the person who gives the party
____	3. stew		c. there are five on your hand
____	4. taste		~~d. ask to come~~
____	5. host		e. meat cooked with vegetables
____	6. guest		f. receiving respect
____	7. honored		g. eat a little

☀ RETELL THE STORY

A. Work with a partner. Student A, retell Eskinder's story. Student B, retell the explanation.

B. What do you think? Share your opinion with your partner.

1. Isaac put food into Lucy's mouth. What did Lucy do? What did Eskinder do? What did Isaac do?

2. Imagine you are in Lucy's situation. What do you do?

3. After this dinner, were Lucy and Isaac angry with Eskinder? Were Eskinder and Isaac still friends?

4. In the future, will Lucy and Isaac be friends?

☀ DICTIONARY DISCOVERIES

The dictionary tells how to say a word. Look at the dictionary information for *good*.

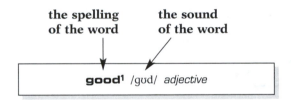

the spelling of the word   the sound of the word

good¹ /gʊd/ *adjective*

Sometimes the spelling and the sound use the same letter. In *good,* the g and d sounds are /g/ and /d/. But sometimes the sound uses a different letter. In *good,* the sound of *oo* is /ʊ/.

Every dictionary has a list of the sounds and their letters. In the *Longman Basic Dictionary of American English,* the list is called the "Pronunciation Table." It is inside the front cover of the dictionary.

Look up these words in your dictionary. Write the sound of *oo* in each word. Practice saying the words with a partner.

  /ʊ/   1. good

_____ 2. food

_____ 3. spoon (noun)

_____ 4. took

_____ 5. scoop (verb)

A. Read the information.

In the United States, most people use knives, forks, and spoons to eat their food. But people also eat some foods with their fingers. Some "finger foods" are corn on the cob, hot dogs, hamburgers, sandwiches, ice cream cones, and sometimes fried chicken.

Very often, people eat with their fingers outdoors. In nice weather, office workers eat lunch outdoors. They buy a sandwich and something to drink. Then they sit in a park and eat their lunch in the sun. On weekends in warm weather, people have picnics. They sit on the grass and eat with their fingers.

B. Work in a small group. Discuss these questions.

1. What foods do Americans eat with their fingers?

2. Where do Americans often eat with their fingers?

CULTURAL EXCHANGE

A. Discuss these questions with a partner.

1. In your culture, or in your family, do people eat with their fingers?

2. What do you eat with your fingers? When? Where?

B. Are these things good manners? Bad manners? Not important? Answer for your culture and other cultures you know about. Work in a group and share what you know. Complete the list with your own ideas.

1. talking with food in your mouth

2. eating with your fingers in a restaurant

3. eating with your left hand

4. eating soup with a spoon

5. eating soup quietly

6. putting both hands on the table while eating

7. taking the last piece of food

8. leaving something on your plate

9. _____

10. _____

 EXPANSION

A. Draw the way your family sets the table for dinner. Show a place for one person. What things go on the table? Where do they go? Explain your drawing to a classmate.

You might show . . .

1. plate(s)
2. glasses or cups
3. extra dishes
4. utensils (knives, forks, spoons, chopsticks, and so on)
5. napkin

B. You ate dinner at someone's home. Write a thank-you note. Use some of these words or choose your own words.

me	last night	fried chicken	delicious
my family	yesterday	Mexican food	excellent
my friend and me	last weekend	sushi	wonderful
		Korean food	great

Dear _____ ,
    (person's name)

   Thank you so much for inviting _____

to your home for dinner _____ . I enjoyed

it very much. I never had _____ before.

Everything was really _____ !

Sincerely,

_____
    (your name)

OUR OWN STORIES

Did you ever see someone use table manners that were different from yours? Tell your classmates about it. Where were you? What did the person do? What did you think about the person?

UNIT 5
Foodways

WHAT DO YOU THINK?

► You invite guests to your home. Do you offer them something to eat or drink? What?

Coffee Break

Read the story.

> My name is Arpi. My family is Armenian, but I grew up in Iran. Now I live in the United States. I am a college student here.
>
> One day, I met some other girls in one of my classes. They were two sisters from Kuwait. Their family was also Armenian. I was happy to meet other Armenians. I wanted to be their friend. I invited them to my home the next day.
>
> When the girls arrived, we began to talk in a very friendly way. They sat down and I immediately brought them cookies and fruit. Then I served them coffee. They looked confused, but I didn't pay much attention. Suddenly, about twenty minutes after they arrived, they stood up. They said goodbye, and they left!

Armenian—From Armenia, a country in western Asia, north of Iran

Can you guess?

Work in a small group. Answer these questions.

► Was Arpi surprised when her guests left? Why did they leave?

► Did Arpi say something wrong?

► Can you think of any other explanation?

Let's find out.

Read the explanation.

> The sisters and Arpi were all Armenian, but they had some different customs. Arpi grew up in Iran. In Iran, people serve coffee to their guests at the beginning of a visit. The sisters grew up in Kuwait. In Kuwait, people serve coffee at the end of a visit. Arpi served coffee and the sisters thought Arpi wanted them to leave. It was very early in the visit, so they felt insulted.
>
> The next day, Arpi spoke to the sisters after class. At first, they didn't want to speak to her. But finally, they explained their custom and Arpi explained hers. Arpi was sorry that her guests felt insulted. She apologized. After this, the three girls became good friends.

Did the explanation surprise you? Why or why not?

A. Read the story and the explanation again. Write the sentences in order.

Arpi apologized.

~~Arpi lived in Iran.~~

Arpi served coffee.

Arpi started college.

The sisters left Arpi's home.

Arpi went to the United States.

Arpi met two Armenian sisters.

The sisters arrived at Arpi's home.

Arpi invited the sisters to her home.

~~Arpi and the sisters became friends.~~

Arpi and the sisters explained their customs.

1. Arpi lived in Iran.

2. _____

3. _____

4. _____

5. _____

6. _____

7. _____

8. _____

9. _____

10. _____

11. Arpi and the sisters became friends.

B. Answer these questions in a small group.

1. The three girls were all Armenian. Why did they have different customs?

2. In Iran and Kuwait, people serve coffee to guests. When do they serve coffee in Iran? When do they serve coffee in Kuwait?

3. Why did the sisters leave after only twenty minutes?

VOCABULARY

What do the underlined words mean? Circle *a* or *b*.

1. I <u>grew up</u> in Iran.

    (a.) was a child and a young woman

    b. was very tall

2. When they <u>arrived</u>, we began to talk.

    a. came

    b. left

3. I <u>immediately</u> served them cookies and fruit.

    a. first

    b. later

4. They looked <u>confused</u>.

    a. comfortable

    b. as if they did not understand

5. I didn't <u>pay much attention</u>.

    a. give them any money

    b. think about it

6. They <u>felt insulted</u>.

    a. thought Arpi didn't like them

    b. were hungry and thirsty

7. Arpi <u>was sorry</u>.

    a. did not understand

    b. was sad

8. Arpi <u>apologized</u>.

    a. said, "I'm sorry"

    b. explained her customs

9. The three girls <u>became</u> good friends.

    a. began to be

    b. liked

RETELL THE STORY

A. Work with a partner. Student A, retell Arpi's story. Student B, retell the explanation.

B. What do you think? Share your opinion with your partner.

1. Who did the right thing? Arpi? The sisters? All of them?

2. Imagine that you are in the sisters' situation (you feel insulted). What do you do?

3. Imagine that you are in Arpi's situation (your guests leave suddenly). What do you do?

DICTIONARY DISCOVERIES

Find these words in your dictionary. Write the left-hand guide word and the right-hand guide word.

	Left-Hand Guide Word	**Right-Hand Guide Word**
1. cookie	consumption	copy
2. sister		
3. friendly		
4. coffee		
5. different		
6. beginning		

A. Read the information.

People come to the United States from all over the world. They bring their favorite foods with them. Some traditional American foods came from other countries. Hamburgers and hot dogs came from Germany. Pizza and spaghetti came from Italy. Donuts came from the Netherlands. Today, many Americans also eat sushi (Japan), tacos (Mexico), and egg rolls (China).

B. Where did these foods come from?

1. donuts   the Netherlands

2. egg rolls   _____

3. hamburgers   _____

4. hot dogs   _____

5. pizza   _____

6. spaghetti   _____

7. sushi   _____

8. tacos   _____

CULTURAL EXCHANGE

A. Answer these questions in a small group. Talk about your family, other people in your culture, and people in other cultures you know about. Work with a group and share what you know.

1. At what age do people begin drinking coffee or tea?

2. When and where do people drink coffee? Tea?

3. What do people usually drink with meals? Water, soda, coffee, tea, milk, or something else?

4. What time do people eat breakfast? Lunch? Dinner?

5. Which is the biggest meal of the day?

6. Do people eat sweets (for example, candy or cake)? When?

B. What is a healthy diet? Americans use this food pyramid. Look at the food pyramid and answer the questions in a small group.

The Food Guide Pyramid: A Guide to Daily Food Choices

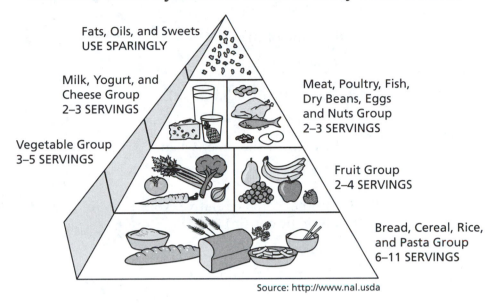

Source: http://www.nal.usda

1. How many food groups are there?

2. Which food group should people eat the most of?

3. Do you know about a culture with different food groups? What are the food groups?

4. Do you think the food pyramid shows a good way to eat? Why or why not?

 EXPANSION

A. Discuss these questions with a partner.

1. Which foods do you like the most?

2. Which foods do you like the least?

3. Which foods do you eat the most?

4. Which foods do you rarely eat?

5. Which foods do you never eat?

6. Which foods do you eat at every meal (breakfast, lunch, and dinner)?

7. Which foods do you always eat at breakfast? At lunch? At dinner?

B. How often does each person in your family cook? Circle *a*, *b*, or *c*. Discuss your answers with a partner.

1. Your mother (or wife)

    a. all of the time

    b. some of the time (when?)

    c. never

2. Your father (or husband)

    a. all of the time

    b. some of the time (when?)

    c. never

3. Another female relative (your grandmother, daughter, sister, aunt, niece, or cousin)

    a. all of the time

    b. some of the time (when?)

    c. never

4. Another male relative (your grandfather, son, brother, uncle, nephew, or cousin)

    a. all of the time

    b. some of the time (when?)

    c. never

5. Someone else (who?)

    a. all of the time

    b. some of the time (when?)

    c. never

OUR OWN STORIES

Tell your classmates about a time when you ate something new to you. Where were you? What was it? Why did you eat it? How did you like it?

UNIT 6
Taking Care of Children

WHAT DO YOU THINK?

► When you were a child, were you ever alone?

► Did people other than your parents ever take care of you? Who were they?

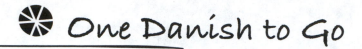
One Danish to Go

Read the story.

> My name is Oskar, and I am from Denmark. Last year, I had a shocking experience. I visited New York City with my daughter, Kirsten. She was fourteen months old. One day, I put Kirsten in her stroller and went to a bank. I wanted to change some money. When we got to the bank, Kirsten was asleep. I went into the bank and left Kirsten outside. I waited in line. Suddenly, two police officers entered the bank. They arrested me!

stroller—A small chair on wheels in which you can push a small child

Can you guess?

Work in a small group. Answer these questions.

► The police arrested Oskar. Why?

► Was there a problem with his visa? Did something happen to Kirsten?

► Can you think of any other explanation?

Let's find out.

Read the explanation.

> Kirsten woke up and began to cry. People worried about her. Two people went into the bank to look for Kirsten's parents. They told Oskar that Kirsten was crying, but Oskar did not bring the baby inside. The people called the police. In New York City, parents cannot leave a small child alone. It is against the law.
>
> But Oskar said that in Denmark, parents often leave their children outside in strollers. The children are safe. Nobody hurts them. Danish people watch out for each other's children. Oskar thought that things were the same in the United States.
>
> After two days, the police learned that Oskar told them the truth. In Denmark, people really do leave their children alone. The police let Oskar go. He went back to Denmark with Kirsten.

Did the explanation surprise you? Why or why not?

✹ COMPREHENSION

A. Read the story and the explanation again. Write _T_ (true) or _F_ (false).

___F___ 1. Oskar was born in the United States.

_____ 2. He visited New York City.

_____ 3. He went into the bank to change some money.

_____ 4. He brought Kirsten inside the bank.

_____ 5. Some people wanted to hurt Kirsten.

_____ 6. The police arrested Oskar.

B. Answer these questions with a partner.

1. Do Danish people leave children alone?
2. Do people in the United States leave children alone?
3. What finally happened to Oskar?

✹ VOCABULARY

Look at the story and the explanation. Write _S_ if the words below are similar. Write _D_ if they are different.

___D___ 1. shocking / good

_____ 2. go into / enter

_____ 3. leave someone alone / go with someone

_____ 4. wait in line / wait alone

_____ 5. inside / outside

_____ 6. watch out for / hurt

_____ 7. arrest someone / let someone go

_____ 8. you cannot do it / it is against the law

✼ RETELL THE STORY

A. Work with a partner. Student A, retell Oskar's story. Student B, retell the explanation.

B. What do you think? Share your opinion with your partner.

1. People told Oskar that Kirsten was crying. Why didn't Oskar bring Kirsten into the bank?

2. The police arrested Oskar. Were they right or wrong?

3. The police kept Oskar for two days. Was that too long or not long enough?

4. Imagine you see a baby alone in a stroller in your town. The baby is crying. What will you do?

✼ DICTIONARY DISCOVERIES

Some words name actions. These words are called *verbs. Put* is a verb. Some words name a person, place, or thing. These words are called *nouns. Money* is a noun. The dictionary tells you if a word is a verb or a noun. It tells you right after the pronunciation.

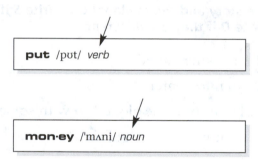

put /pʊt/ *verb*

mon·ey /ˈmʌni/ *noun*

Some words are both verbs and nouns. The dictionary lists them twice— once as a verb and once as a noun.

> **vis·it¹** /ˈvɪzɪt/ *verb*
> **1** to go and see a person or place: *We visited our friends in town.*
> **2** to talk to someone in a friendly way: *I visited **with** Kathy for an hour.*
>
> **visit²** *noun*
> the act of going and seeing a person or place: *We had a visit **from** your teacher.*

Work with a partner. Look in the dictionary. Are these words verbs or nouns? Or are they both? Write V (verb), N (noun), or V + N (both).

_V + N_ 1. bank

_____ 2. bring

_____ 3. child

_____ 4. experience

_____ 5. leave

▲ CULTURE CAPSULE

A. Read the information.

In most places in the United States, it is against the law for parents to leave small children alone. What do working parents do? Sometimes grandparents or other family members take care of small children. Or parents pay a babysitter to watch their children. Some parents leave their children at a day care center. At a day care center, many children can play together.

Some school children go to a relative's house or to a neighbor's house after school. Other children go to clubs or to other places where adults can watch them. Parents get their children after work.

B. Discuss these questions with a partner.

1. In the United States, sometimes both parents work. Who takes care of their small children?

2. Where can school children go after school?

CULTURAL EXCHANGE

A. What do you know about child care in the United States and other countries? Work with a group and share what you know. Write the names of the other countries. Write *yes* or *no* for each custom.

Custom	United States	Denmark	_____	_____
It's OK to leave small children alone.	no	yes		
Most mothers stay home with their children.				
Babysitters take care of children.				
Family members take care of children.				
There are day care centers.				
There are places for children to go after school.				

B. Discuss these questions with a partner.

In your family or your culture . . .

1. Can children walk to school alone? At what age?

2. Can children choose their own clothes? At what age?

3. Can children choose their own friends?

4. Do parents give children money? How much? What things can the children buy?

5. Do children help in the house? What work do they do?

EXPANSION

A. All parents want their children to be good. Many American parents reward their children when they behave well. Sometimes the children get gold stars on a list. What is a "gold star" in your family?

Make a list of good behavior for a child in your family. Use your own paper.

Example:

Kerry - Good Behavior Today

☆ Brushed his teeth

☆ Made his bed

☆ Went to bed at nine o'clock

B. Discuss your answers in a small group. Think about how your parents raised you. What did you like about the way they raised you? What didn't you like? What would you change raising your own children?

OUR OWN STORIES

Tell your classmates about a time when your parents left you alone. Or tell about a time you had a problem with your parent or your child.

UNIT 7
Verbal Customs

WHAT DO YOU THINK?

► Did anyone ever break a promise to you?

► Is is ever OK to break a promise? When?

✳ Maybe Yes, Maybe No

Read the story.

> I am a writer. My name is Julie. I am writing a book about wedding customs all over the world. I have an acquaintance named Shyla. She is a dancer. She lives in the United States, but she is from India. I interviewed Shyla about Indian weddings. She told me about Indian wedding clothes and gifts. I took a lot of notes.
>
> After the interview, I thanked Shyla. I asked her if she would correct my notes. Shyla said yes. She told me to mail my notes to her when I finished writing them.
>
> I put my notes in an envelope and mailed them to Shyla the next day. I waited two weeks, but she never sent them back to me. I called her, and she apologized. I asked her again to mail back the corrected notes. She said yes, but nothing happened. I waited a few more weeks and called again. Again she said yes, but I never received the notes from her. After that, I was too angry to call her again.

Can you guess?

Work in a small group. Answer these questions.

► Shyla did not correct Julie's notes. Why not?

► Did she forget?

► Can you think of any other explanation?

Let's find out.

Read the explanation.

> Shyla promised to read Julie's notes and correct them. But she did not mean what she said. Shyla had to get ready for a dance performance. She had to teach the other dancers. She had to make the costumes. She was doing everything herself. She did not have time to read Julie's notes. Julie's request was impossible for Shyla.
>
> Shyla said yes because she didn't want to say no. In Shyla's culture, it is bad manners to say no to requests.

Did the explanation surprise you? Why or why not?

COMPREHENSION

A. Read the story and the explanation again. Write _J_ (Julie) or _S_ (Shyla).

___S___ 1. She is from India.

_____ 2. She is a writer.

_____ 3. She answered questions about weddings.

_____ 4. She promised to correct the notes.

_____ 5. She was very busy.

_____ 6. She was angry.

B. Answer these questions in a small group.

1. Did Shyla have time to correct Julie's notes?

2. Why did Shyla say yes?

3. Did Julie understand Shyla?

VOCABULARY

What do these sentences mean? Circle _a_ or _b_.

1. I have an <u>acquaintance</u> named Shyla.

   a. Shyla is a stranger.

   (b.) I know Shyla.

2. I <u>interviewed</u> Shyla about weddings.

   a. I asked her questions.

   b. I met her and said hello.

3. I <u>took notes</u>.

   a. Shyla gave me books.

   b. I wrote down information.

4. I <u>mailed</u> her my notes the next day.

   a. I read them to her.

   b. I sent them to her.

5. <u>Nothing happened</u>.

    a. Shyla did not send the notes back.

    b. I never saw Shyla again.

6. I <u>never received</u> the notes.

    a. The notes did not come back.

    b. The notes were not correct.

7. Shyla <u>promised</u> to read the notes.

    a. She said, "I will read them."

    b. She said, "I'm sorry. I don't have time."

8. She was doing everything <u>herself</u>.

    a. People were helping her.

    b. She was working alone.

9. Julie's request was <u>impossible</u> for Shyla.

    a. Shyla could do what Julie wanted.

    b. Shyla could not do what Julie wanted.

RETELL THE STORY

A. Work with a partner. Student A, retell Julie's story. Student B, retell the explanation.

B. What do you think? Share your opinion with your partner.

1. Imagine that you are in Shyla's situation (you don't have time to correct the notes). What do you do?

2. Imagine that you are in Julie's situation (you called Shyla twice). What do you do?

DICTIONARY DISCOVERIES

Generally, to make a singular noun plural, you add –s:

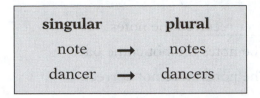

singular		plural
note	→	notes
dancer	→	dancers

If the plural is regular (if you add –s), the dictionary says nothing. But for some plural forms, you have to do something different. The dictionary tells you what to do.

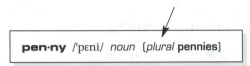

pen·ny /ˈpɛni/ *noun* [*plural* **pennies**]

Look up these singular nouns. Write their plural forms.

Singular	Plural
1. promise	promises
2. story	
3. day	
4. herself	
5. request	
6. woman	
7. movie	

A. Read the information.

In the United States, questions are often very direct: "Do you like this?" "Will you do that?" Americans want direct answers too. They believe that "Yes" means yes and "No" means no. They do not like indirect answers. Often, they do not understand them.

But Americans are not direct about everything. There are some things that Americans don't talk about with people they don't know well. With acquaintances, many Americans don't like to discuss religion or politics. Americans don't ask how old people are (except children). Americans don't talk about how much money they make or how much they paid for something.

B. Discuss these questions with a partner.

1. Do Americans believe "Yes" means yes? Does "Yes" mean yes in other cultures you know about?

2. Americans don't like to talk about some things with people they don't know well. What are some of these things?

CULTURAL EXCHANGE

A. Can people ask these questions in your culture? Make a check (✔) under *Nobody, Acquaintance,* or *Friend.*

Who Can You Ask?	Nobody	Acquaintance	Friend
1. How old are you?	☐	☐	☐
2. Why aren't you married?	☐	☐	☐
3. Why don't you have children?	☐	☐	☐
4. Where do you work?	☐	☐	☐
5. What do you do?	☐	☐	☐
6. How much money do you make?	☐	☐	☐
7. How much did your sweater cost?	☐	☐	☐
8. How much did your house cost?	☐	☐	☐
9. What religion are you?	☐	☐	☐
10. Who are you going to vote for?	☐	☐	☐

B. Technology has changed verbal customs in many ways. Now there are new manners to think about.

What are good manners when you use cell phones (mobile phones)? Look at situations 1–8. For each situation, answer questions a–e. Discuss your answers in a small group.

Situations

1. You are walking alone on a city street.

2. You are walking with a friend on a city street.

3. You are driving a car.

4. You are eating with a friend in a restaurant.

5. You are watching a movie in a movie theater.

6. You are at school or at work.

Questions

a. Is your phone turned on?

b. If it is, do you answer it?

c. How long do you talk?

d. Do you try to speak quietly?

e. Do you apologize? To whom?

 EXPANSION

A. Look at the pictures and complete the crossword puzzle. The words are in the story "Maybe Yes, Maybe No."

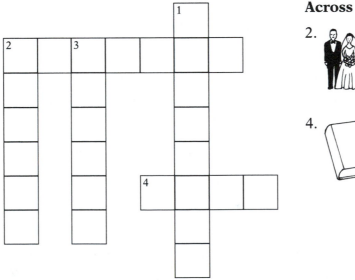

Across

2.

4.

Down

1.

2.

3.

B. Interview a classmate about a trip he or she took. Take notes below.

Who? _____

(the person's name)

What? _____

(vacation? business trip? honeymoon?)

Where? _____

When? _____

Why? _____

(Why did he or she choose that place?)

OUR OWN STORIES

Did you ever break a promise? What did you promise to do? Who did you make the promise to? Why did you break the promise? What happened?

The Hidden Meaning of Colors

WHAT DO YOU THINK?

➤ What is your favorite color?

➤ Is there a color you never wear? What is it?

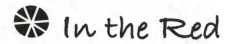 In the Red

Read the story.

> My name is Ed. I manage a college bookstore. Once a year, students can bring their old textbooks to the bookstore. We buy the used books from the students. Later, we sell them again for a very low price.
>
> This year I asked my student aide, Jim, to help me. Jim sat at a table and took the students' books. The students had to sign their names on a form. Then they took the form to the cashier. The cashier gave them money.
>
> Most of the students signed the forms and got their money. But some students just stood at the table. They looked upset. They didn't sign the forms. Jim was puzzled. He asked me what was wrong.

student aide—A college student who has a part-time job in the college

Can you guess?

Work in a small group. Answer these questions.

► The students did not sign the forms. Why not?

► Did they not want the money?

► Can you think of any other explanation?

Let's find out.

Read the explanation.

> Jim put some pens on the table for the students to use. They were red pens. Some of the students were Korean Buddhists. These students were upset. In their culture, they write a person's name in red when the person dies. These students did not want to sign their names in red. Signing their names in red was like asking for death.
>
> Ed explained the students' problem to Jim. Immediately, Jim removed the red pens. He put blue pens on the table. The students were relieved. They signed their names in blue and got their money.

Buddhists—People who believe in the teachings of Buddha

Did the explanation surprise you? Why or why not?

✿ COMPREHENSION

A. Read the story and the explanation again. Write the sentences in order.

The Korean Buddhist students got their money.

Jim put blue pens on the table.

Some of the students didn't sign the forms.

Jim asked Ed to explain.

Jim put red pens on the table.

~~Ed asked Jim to help him.~~

The students signed the forms in blue.

Ed explained the Korean Buddhist custom to Jim.

1. Ed asked Jim to help him.

2. _____

3. _____

4. _____

5. _____

6. _____

7. _____

8. _____

B. Answer these questions with a partner.

1. What did a name in red mean to Jim?

2. What does a name in red mean to Korean Buddhists?

3. How did Jim solve the problem for the students?

What do the underlined words mean? Circle *a* or *b*.

1. I <u>manage</u> a college bookstore.

   (a.) direct the business of

   b. work at

2. We buy <u>used</u> books.

   a. new

   b. old

3. We sell the books for <u>a very low price</u>.

   a. a lot of money

   b. not much money

4. The students had to <u>sign their names on a form</u>.

   a. write their names on a piece of paper

   b. write their names in red

5. They looked <u>upset</u>.

   a. happy

   b. unhappy

6. Jim <u>was puzzled</u>.

   a. didn't understand

   b. was angry

7. You do it when the person <u>dies</u>.

   a. begins living

   b. stops living

8. It was like asking for <u>death</u>.

   a. the beginning of their lives

   b. the end of their lives

9. The students <u>were relieved</u>.

   a. felt better

   b. felt worse

RETELL THE STORY

A. **Work with a partner. Student A, retell Ed's story. Student B, retell the explanation.**

B. **What do you think? Share your opinion with your partner.**

1. The students didn't explain their problem to Jim. Why not?

2. Imagine that you are in the students' situation (you don't want to sign your name in red). What do you do?

3. Imagine that you are in Jim's situation (the students aren't signing the forms). What do you do?

DICTIONARY DISCOVERIES

To change a verb from the present tense to the past tense, you usually add *–ed*:

present		past
they sign	→	they signed
they look	→	they looked

But some verbs don't have an *–ed* ending. The dictionary tells you the correct form for the past tense.

sit /sɪt/ *verb* (**sitting**, *past tense* **sat**, *past participle* **sat**)

The past tense of *sit* is *sat*.

Look up these verbs in the dictionary. Write the past tense of each verb.

1. take   took

2. have   _____

3. give   _____

4. get   _____

5. stand   _____

6. put   _____

7. write   _____

A. Read the information.

Some colors have special meanings in the United States. Wedding dresses are white because white means goodness and purity. Babies and children also wear white at special times. Black makes people think about death. People wear black clothing to funerals.

Colors can have more than one meaning. In the United States, a day when good things happen is a "red-letter day." Red roses mean love. But teachers use red pens to show mistakes on students' papers. And when a business is "in the red," it is losing money.

B. Write *T* (true) or *F* (false).

In the United States, . . .

_____ 1. White is for good things.   _____ 4. Black is for bad things.

_____ 2. White is for bad things.   _____ 5. Red is for good things.

_____ 3. Black is for good things.   _____ 6. Red is for bad things.

❊ CULTURAL EXCHANGE

A. What do different colors mean in the countries you know about? Work in groups and share what you know. Write the names of other colors and countries. Write the meaning of each color.

Color	Meaning in the United States	Meaning in _____	Meaning in _____
White			
Black			
Red			
_____			
_____			

The Hidden Meaning of Colors **57**

B. Answer these questions and discuss your answers with a partner.

1. Do you like to wear bright colors (pink, yellow, red, bright blue, and so on)? When? Where?

2. Do you like to wear dark colors (black, brown, gray, dark blue, and so on)? When? Where?

3. What is your favorite color for clothing?

4. What is your favorite color for a bedroom? For a car? For a house?

5. What colors do you like for eyes (black, brown, green, blue, gray)?

6. What colors do you like for hair? Black, brown, blond, gray, or white? Blue, green, orange, or purple?

 EXPANSION

A. Find these colors in the word square. Circle the words.

BLUE	BLACK	GREEN	ORANGE
RED	~~YELLOW~~	WHITE	

The words go four ways: right →   left ←   down ↓   up ↑

```
Ⓨ  E  L  L  O  Ⓦ
 G  D  K  F  R  E
 R  E  C  Z  A  T
 E  R  A  O  N  I
 E  U  L  B  G  H
 N  C  B  K  E  W
```

B. Work in groups. Think of new names for colors. Share your color names with the whole class. Which names are the best?

Examples: Grass green, chalk white

OUR OWN STORIES

What is your favorite color? Why do you like it? Do you own something that color? Tell your classmates.

UNIT 9

Greetings

WHAT DO YOU THINK?

► How do you greet your mother?

► How do you greet a friend?

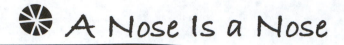

A Nose Is a Nose

Read the story.

> Let me introduce myself. My name is Ben. I was on a business trip in New Zealand. At the airport, I watched families greet each other. Some shook hands. Some hugged and kissed. Some were happy. Some were serious.
>
> One man arrived from a trip. He looked like a businessman. He wore a dark suit and he carried a leather briefcase. Another man was there to greet him. They did not shake hands or hug. They pressed their noses together. I was surprised, but this greeting looked very natural for the two men.

Can you guess?

Work in a small group. Answer these questions.

► The two men pressed their noses together. Why? What were they doing?

Let's find out.

Read the explanation.

> The traveler and his friend were Maori. When two Maori people greet each other, they press one nose against the other nose. They call this gesture a *hongi*. When two people press noses they share the same breath. This unites them. The *hongi* means friendship and respect. Some people of Alaska and Canada also press their noses together to greet each other.

Maori—The original people of New Zealand

Did the explanation surprise you? Why or why not?

COMPREHENSION

A. Read the story and the explanation again. Write *T* (true) or *F* (false).

___F___ 1. Ben is from New Zealand.

_____ 2. Ben was in New Zealand.

_____ 3. Ben saw people in an airport.

_____ 4. Ben saw two men saying goodbye.

_____ 5. The two men were from Canada.

_____ 6. Ben saw many *hongis* in the airport.

_____ 7. Ben was surprised.

B. Answer these questions in a small group.

1. What people greet each other with a *hongi*?
2. What does the *hongi* mean?
3. What does a *hongi* look like?

VOCABULARY

What do the underlined words mean? Circle *a* or *b*.

1. People <u>greeted</u> each other.
   - (a.) said hello to
   - b. walked away from

2. People <u>were serious</u>.
   - a. showed happiness
   - b. did not show happiness

3. Ben was <u>on a trip</u>.
   - a. on an airplane
   - b. away from home

4. He <u>carried</u> a briefcase.
   - a. had it in his hand
   - b. put it on the floor

5. They <u>pressed</u> their noses together.

    a. showed

    b. touched

6. It looked <u>natural</u> for them.

    a. normal, usual

    b. strange, unusual

7. The <u>traveler</u> was Maori.

    a. person waiting for someone

    b. person going to a place far away

8. They <u>share</u> the same breath.

    a. have it together

    b. have it alone

9. The *hongi* <u>unites them</u>.

    a. brings them together

    b. makes them alone

10. The *hongi* means <u>respect</u>.

    a. a bad opinion, disgust

    b. a good opinion, honor

RETELL THE STORY

A. Work with a partner. Student A, retell Ben's story. Student B, retell the explanation.

B. What do you think? Share your opinion with your partner.

1. You are in New Zealand. Someone greets you with a *hongi*. What do you do?

2. You are at home. Someone greets you with a *hongi*. What do you do?

DICTIONARY DISCOVERIES

When you want to write the *–ing* form of a verb, usually you just add *–ing* to it:

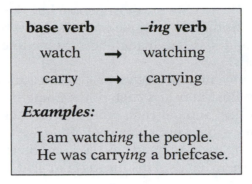

base verb		*–ing* verb
watch	➡	watching
carry	➡	carrying

Examples:

I am watch*ing* the people.
He was carry*ing* a briefcase.

But sometimes the spelling is different. The dictionary tells you the correct spelling.

shake /ʃeɪk/ *verb* (**shaking,** *past tense* **shook,** *past participle* **shaken**)

The *–ing* form of *shake* does not use the *–e* at the end of the word. The *–ing* form is *shaking.*

Look up these words in your dictionary. Write the special *–ing* forms.

1. introduce   introducing

2. arrive   _____

3. share   _____

4. hug   _____

5. get   _____

6. die   _____

A. Read the information.

In the United States, most people hug, kiss, or shake hands to greet each other. Sometimes people just say "Hi" when they meet. Americans often hug and kiss family members. Sometimes they also hug and kiss close friends.

Generally, men don't hug or kiss other men. But men originally from the Middle East may kiss each other. Sometimes men from Latin America hug each other and pat each other on the back.

People who do not know each other well usually shake hands. Businesspeople shake hands too. When Americans see someone far away, they wave their hands. This means "I'm glad to see you."

B. Discuss these questions with a partner.

1. How do most Americans greet family members and close friends?

2. How do they greet other people?

3. Do men ever hug and kiss each other? Who? When?

CULTURAL EXCHANGE

A. What greetings do most people in your culture use? What greetings do you use? Fill in the chart on page 65. Use the key below. Share your answers with a group.

	Key
KM	= **Kiss the mouth**
KF	= **Kiss the face**
KH	= **Kiss the hand**
H	= **Hug**
SH	= **Shake hands**
B	= **Bow**
S	= **Speak (what do you say?)**
O	= **Other (what?)**
NA	= **Not applicable (you don't greet this person)**

To Greet	Most People in My Culture	Me
Grandfather		
Grandmother		
Father		
Mother		
Brother or sister		
Husband or wife		
Your baby		
A stranger's baby		
Friend		
Someone you are meeting for the first time		
Personal acquaintance		
Business acquaintance		
Your teacher		
Your boss		

B. Work in a group. How do people say goodbye? Match the words in *A* with the languages and countries in *B*. Then add more goodbye words, languages, and countries that you know.

	A		B
_c_	1. Goodbye		a. French / Canada
___	2. Ciao		b. Hebrew / Israel
___	3. Hasta luego		~~c. English / Canada~~
___	4. Sayonara		d. Arabic / Saudi Arabia
___	5. Au revoir		e. Japanese / Japan
___	6. Do svidanja		f. Italian / Italy
___	7. Shalom aleichem		g. Russian / Russia
___	8. Es-salaam aleikum		h. Spanish / Mexico
___	9. _____		i. _____
___	10. _____		j. _____
___	11. _____		k. _____

A. Imagine that you are a world traveler. Practice these greetings with your classmates.

B. Unscramble these words. All the words are in "A Nose Is a Nose."

1. esson (plural noun)   <u>noses</u>

2. sidesk (past tense verb)   _____

3. ghedug (past tense verb)   _____

4. potrair (noun)   _____

5. stinggere (plural noun)   _____

6. creefbias (noun)   _____

 OUR OWN STORIES

Did you ever greet someone in the wrong way? Or did someone ever greet you in the wrong way? Tell your story.

UNIT 10
Weddings

WHAT DO YOU THINK?

► Did you ever go to a wedding of people from another culture? What happened?

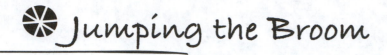

Jumping the Broom

Read the story.

Irish-American—
Mickey is American.
His family
originally came
from Ireland.

African-American
Ted is American.
His family
originally came
from Africa.

minister—A
religious leader in a
Christian church

> My name is Ted. I live near Chicago. I work in an electronics store at the mall. A friend works there with me. His name is Mickey and he is Irish-American. I am African-American. My sweetheart, Gail, and I got married. We invited Mickey to the wedding.
>
> It was a beautiful wedding. The church was filled with flowers. Gail wore a long white dress. I wore a tuxedo. All the guests were in formal clothes too, including Mickey.
>
> After the minister said, "You are now husband and wife," we kissed. Then my sister came to the front of the church. She put a plain old broom on the floor in front of us. In our formal wedding clothes, Gail and I jumped over the broom. I looked at Mickey. He was trying to be polite, but he looked so surprised. I had to laugh!

Can you guess?

Work in a small group. Answer these questions.

► Ted and Gail jumped over a broom. Why?

► Did Ted and Gail hope their house would always be clean?

► Can you think of any other explanation?

Let's find out.

Read the explanation.

slavery—From
1600 to 1865,
white people in
the United States
could own African
people. The
Africans worked
for them without
pay as slaves.

> Ted and Gail were following an old African-American wedding custom. It goes back to the time of slavery. Slaves could not get married in church. Jumping over the broom was a way to marry without a church or a minister. Ted and Gail were honoring their African-American ancestors. The broom was from Ted's family. His parents and grandparents jumped over it at their weddings.
>
> Irish-Americans do not have the same custom. Ted knew Mickey would be surprised. He was waiting to see Mickey's face when they jumped over the broom.

Did the explanation surprise you? Why or why not?

COMPREHENSION

A. Read the story and the explanation again. Write the sentences in order.

Ted and Gail invited Mickey to their wedding.

Mickey looked surprised.

Ted and Mickey became friends.

The wedding began.

~~The wedding ended.~~

Ted laughed.

Ted and Gail were husband and wife.

~~Slavery ended.~~

Ted and Gail jumped over the broom.

Ted's grandparents jumped over the broom.

1. Slavery ended. _____

2. _____

3. _____

4. _____

5. _____

6. _____

7. _____

8. _____

9. _____

10. The wedding ended. _____

B. Answer these questions with a partner

1. Why did Gail and Ted jump over the broom?
2. Why was Mickey surprised?

VOCABULARY
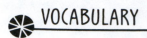

Look at the story and the explanation. Match the words in *A* with the meanings in *B*.

	A	**B**
_e_	1. get married	a. a brush for cleaning the floor
___	2. wedding	b. not having
___	3. tuxedo	c. clothes people wear to important ceremonies and parties
___	4. polite	d. with good manners
___	5. broom	~~e. become husband and wife~~
___	6. formal clothes	f. family members who lived long ago
___	7. jump	g. use your feet to push yourself off the floor
___	8. without	h. a ceremony that makes two people husband and wife
___	9. ancestors	i. a man's formal black suit

DICTIONARY DISCOVERIES

Sometimes the dictionary gives you an example of the word in a sentence.

> **plain¹** /pleɪn/ *adjective*
> **1** simple; without a pattern on it: *He wore a plain blue suit.*

Circle these words in "Jumping the Broom." Look up each word in your dictionary. Write the definition. Write the example sentence that you find in your dictionary. Do any of your classmates have different dictionaries? Write their example sentences too.

1. formal (adjective)

   Meaning: _____

   Examples: _____

   _____

2. invite (verb)

   Meaning: _____

   Examples: _____

   _____

3. slave (noun)

   Meaning: _____

   Examples: _____

   _____

RETELL THE STORY

A. Work with a partner. Student A, retell Ted's story. Student B, retell the explanation.

B. What do you think? Share your opinion with your partner.

1. Why did Ted laugh?
2. Are Mickey and Ted good friends?
3. African-Americans remember the time of slavery at their weddings. Is this a good idea?

A. Read the information.

In the United States, many weddings follow the same customs. Before the wedding, the groom cannot see the bride in her wedding dress. It's bad luck. Traditionally, a bride wears a white dress. She also wears "something old, something new, something borrowed, and something blue."

After the wedding, the guests throw rice (not cooked!) at the bride and groom. Later, the bride throws her flowers to the unmarried women at the wedding. The woman who catches the flowers will be the next bride.

The next day, the couple usually goes away together. This wedding trip is called a *honeymoon*. In the past, the honeymoon was the first time a couple was alone together. It was a time for them to get to know each other without their families.

B. Work in a small group. Discuss these questions.

1. What brings bad luck on a wedding day?

2. What does the bride wear?

3. What does the bride throw?

4. What do the guests throw?

5. What is a honeymoon?

❊ CULTURAL EXCHANGE

A. Talk about weddings in your culture and other cultures you know about. Work with a group. Answer the questions.

1. What does the bride wear? What does the groom wear? Do other people in the wedding wear special clothes?

2. Do the bride and groom go on a honeymoon? Are there popular places to go on a honeymoon?

3. What traditional customs do people follow?

B. Who does these things in families in your culture? In your family? Write *H* (husband), *W* (wife), or *B* (both).

Who in the Family . . .	My Culture Traditionally	My Culture Now	My Family
Earns the money?			
Pays the bills?			
Chooses where the family will live?			
Chooses the family's food, clothing, etc.?			
Chooses the family's house, car, etc.?			
Takes care of the children?			

EXPANSION

A. Imagine you are on your honeymoon. Complete the postcard with words from the list, or use your own words.

London	exciting	great	perfect	to the beach
Hawaii	interesting	wonderful	rainy	dancing
Paris	beautiful	fabulous	hot	to the movies

Dear _____,
       (person's name)

We are on our honeymoon in _____.

It is very _____, and we are

having a _____ time. The weather

is _____. Yesterday we went

_____. We'll be home on Sunday.

See you soon!

Love,

_____
   (your name)

To: _____

_____

_____

_____
(person's name and address)

B. A friend is getting married. Make suggestions for a happy marriage. Work with a partner. Then, share your suggestions with the class.

1. Is your friend a man or a woman?

_____

2. What should your friend always do?

_____

_____

3. What should your friend never do?

_____

_____

 OUR OWN STORIES

Were you ever surprised at a wedding? Tell your story. Or tell how you or your family honor your ancestors.

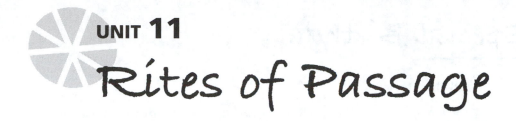

UNIT 11
Rites of Passage

WHAT DO YOU THINK?

► When does a child become an adult?

► Do people ever celebrate on the day a child becomes an adult? Did you ever go to this kind of celebration?

✳ Special Birthday

Read the story.

> My name is Wilf. I am a photographer from London, England. Last year, I went to the United States to take photographs of city parks. One Saturday, I was at Central Park in New York City. I noticed a large, happy group of people taking photographs in front of a fountain.
>
> It was a charming scene—green grass, the falling water of the fountain, and eight very pretty young women. One of the young women wore a long white dress. She had flowers in her hair. The other young women wore pink.
>
> I started taking photographs, too. I spoke to one of the people near me. "Did the wedding just finish?" He looked at me strangely and he asked, "What wedding?"

Can you guess?

Work in a small group. Answer these questions.

► Wilf thought the people were part of a wedding. Did you think so, too?

► Can you think of any other explanation?

Let's find out.

Read the explanation.

> The celebration was for the young woman in white. It was her fifteenth birthday. Her family was originally from Mexico. Their celebration was a *quinceañera*. This is the time when Mexican, Cuban, Puerto Rican, and other Central American girls traditionally become adults. A *quinceañera* looks like a wedding. People wear formal clothes. There are many guests and there is a special cake. But there is no groom!

Did the explanation surprise you? Why or why not?

COMPREHENSION

A. Read the story and the explanation again. Write _T_ (true) or _F_ (false).

__F__ 1. Wilf lived in New York City.

_____ 2. Wilf was a photographer.

_____ 3. He saw a wedding party by a fountain.

_____ 4. The young woman in white was the bride.

_____ 5. The young woman was fifteen years old.

_____ 6. The young woman's family came from Mexico.

_____ 7. A _quinceañera_ is the same as a wedding.

_____ 8. A _quinceañera_ is a custom from Mexico, Puerto Rico, Cuba, and other Central American countries.

B. Answer these questions in a small group.

1. Why did Wilf think it was a wedding?

2. How do people celebrate _quinceañeras_?

3. Why do people celebrate _quinceañeras_?

VOCABULARY

Look at the story and the explanation. Write _S_ if the words below are similar. Write _D_ if they are different.

__S__ 1. noticed / saw

_____ 2. charming / beautiful

_____ 3. fountain / river

_____ 4. celebrating / having a party for

_____ 5. originally / in the beginning

_____ 6. observing / forgetting about

_____ 7. popular / not liked

_____ 8. adult / grown-up

RETELL THE STORY

A. **Work with a partner. Student A, retell Wilf's story. Student B, retell the explanation.**

B. **What do you think? Share your opinion with your partner.**

1. Wilf began taking pictures. He did not ask anyone first. Was this OK?

2. Is it a good idea to have a celebration when a teenager becomes an adult?

3. When do girls become adults? At about age fifteen? At another age? How about boys?

DICTIONARY DISCOVERIES

Some words describe a person, place, or thing. They are called *adjectives*. The dictionary tells you if a word is an adjective.

> **hap·py** /ˈhæpi/ *adjective* (happier, happiest)
> **1** feeling very pleased: *I am happy to see you again.* ➤➤ opposite UNHAPPY
> **2 Happy Birthday!, Happy New Year!** said to someone to wish him or her good luck on a special occasion

Look up these words in your dictionary. Write *Y* (yes) if the word is an adjective. Write *N* (no) if the word is not an adjective.

_Y_ 1. central

____ 2. wedding

____ 3. charming

____ 4. young

____ 5. pretty

____ 6. special

A. Read the information.

When do children become adults? In the United States, people can drive a car at age fifteen or sixteen. Many teenagers feel they are adults when they can drive. Usually, parents do not agree. They do not think their children are adults yet.

At age seventeen, young people can join the army without their parents' permission. But most people believe that young people become adults at age eighteen. This is when people usually graduate from high school. It is when most people go to college or get a full-time job. It is also when people can vote. And in most states, people must be eighteen years old to get married without their parents' permission.

Almost everyone agrees that a person is an adult when he or she gets a job, gets married, or moves out of his or her parents' home.

B. Discuss these questions with a partner.

1. When can young people in the United States drive?

2. When do they usually graduate from high school?

3. When can they join the army without their parents' permission?

4. When can they vote?

5. When can they get married without their parents' permission?

CULTURAL EXCHANGE

A. Answer these questions in a small group. Talk about your culture or your family.

1. When does a child become an adult? Is there a special celebration? What do people do?

2. Are some birthdays more important than others? Which ones? Why are they important?

3. How do you celebrate birthdays? Where do you go? What do you do? Who celebrates with you?

B. Write answers about special occasions in your family. Add other occasions that are important to you. Then work with a group and share what you know.

Occasion	How Do You Celebrate It?
Graduation (you finish school)	
Engagement (you promise to marry someone)	
Wedding anniversary (every year, you celebrate the day you got married)	
Moving into your first home	
Retirement (you stop working for the rest of your life)	

 EXPANSION

A. You are a parent. Your child is now an adult. What will you say to him or her? Share your ideas with a partner.

Now you can . . .

1. _____

2. _____

Now you have to . . .

1. _____

2. _____

B. Work with a partner. Plan a celebration for one of your classmates. Add more things to think about. Then tell the classmate your plans.

Things to Think About	Notes
The occasion	
The time and place	
The guests	
Food, music	

 OUR OWN STORIES

Tell your classmates about a special celebration in your life. When was it? What was the occasion? Who was there? What happened?

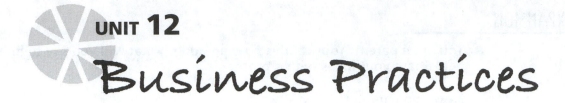

Business Practices

WHAT DO YOU THINK?

▶ Do you have a business card?

▶ What do you do with business cards you receive?

Carrying Cards

Read the story.

> My name is Shig Ito. I live in Tokyo and I sell computers. One day, I went to a school where people learn English. I talked to the computer teacher, Mr. Wilson, about new computers for the school.
>
> Mr. Wilson was from California. He was new to Japan, but he could speak a little Japanese. I handed him my business card. He took the card with one hand. With the other hand, he took a pen out of his pocket. Then, when I told him the computer prices, he wrote down the information on my card. I was surprised and insulted.

Can you guess?

Work in a small group. Answer these questions.

► Mr. Ito was surprised and insulted. Why?

► Did Mr. Wilson complain about the computer prices?

► Can you think of any other explanation?

Let's find out.

Read the explanation.

> In Japan, there are strict rules for giving and taking business cards. Japanese people use both hands to give business cards to others. Japanese people also use both hands to take business cards. In Japan, people look at business cards carefully. Then they put the business cards away. People never put business cards in a back pocket. People never write on business cards. Mr. Wilson insulted Mr. Ito when he accepted the business card with one hand. He also insulted Mr. Ito when he wrote on the business card.
>
> Mr. Wilson did not mean to insult Mr. Ito. He spoke some Japanese, but he did not know Japanese customs about business cards. Americans do not have strict rules about business cards. Americans give or take business cards with either hand. Americans may write on business cards. They keep business cards anywhere that is convenient.

Did the explanation surprise you? Why or why not?

A. Read the story and the explanation again. Write *W* (Mr. Wilson), *I* (Mr. Ito), or *B* (both).

___I___ 1. He sells computers.

_____ 2. He lives in Tokyo.

_____ 3. He is from California.

_____ 4. He is a computer teacher.

_____ 5. He speaks Japanese.

_____ 6. He gave his card to the other man.

_____ 7. He took the card with one hand.

_____ 8. He wrote prices on the card.

_____ 9. He was surprised and insulted.

_____ 10. He insulted the other man.

_____ 11. He uses two hands to give and take business cards.

B. Answer these questions with a partner.

1. What did Mr. Ito expect?

2. What did Mr. Wilson do wrong?

3. What else does Mr. Wilson need to know?

VOCABULARY

Look at the story and the explanation. Match the words in *A* with the meanings in *B*.

A	B
_f_ 1. handed	a. easy
___ 2. strict rules	b. the left hand or the right hand
___ 3. back pocket	c. want, intend
___ 4. accepted	d. a place to keep things, on the back of your pants
___ 5. mean	e. clear, correct ways to do things
___ 6. either hand	f. ~~gave~~
___ 7. convenient	g. took

DICTIONARY DISCOVERIES

Some words have more than one meaning. For these words, the dictionary gives two or more meanings. *Business* has two meanings.

> **busi·ness** /'bɪznɪs/ *noun*
> **1** a company that provides service or sells things to earn money: *He has a furniture business in town.*
> **2** (U) making, buying, and selling things, or the amount of money made doing this: *Business is very good this year.* (=we are earning a lot of money)

Look up these words in your dictionary. Write two meanings for each word.

1. pen _____

_____

2. name _____

_____

3. say _____

_____

RETELL THE STORY

A. Work with a partner. Student A, retell Mr. Ito's story. Student B, retell the explanation.

B. What do you think? Share your opinion with your partner.

1. Mr. Wilson is new to Japan. Should Mr. Ito forgive him?

2. Imagine Mr. Wilson learns about business card customs. Should he apologize to Mr. Ito?

3. Imagine you are Mr. Wilson's boss. Mr. Wilson is going to meet with a Japanese computer salesperson. What do you do?

A. Read the information.

Americans have strict rules about time in business. It is important to be on time. A meeting that is scheduled for 10 A.M. really starts at 10 A.M. You should get to meetings a few minutes early. If you cannot be at a meeting, you should call the other people and tell them. This shows respect for the other people at the meeting. You should also call if you will be late.

Most business offices are open Monday through Friday from 9 A.M. to 5 P.M. Every day, workers usually take one hour for lunch and two ten-minute breaks. Most workers get from five to fourteen paid holidays. Workers usually get two weeks of paid vacation each year.

B. Work in a small group. Answer these questions about business in the United States.

1. You have a meeting at 3:00. What time do you need to be there?

2. You are going to be late for a meeting. What do you do? Why?

3. How much free time do most office workers have in a workday?

4. How many paid days off do most office workers have every year?

CULTURAL EXCHANGE

A. Work in a group. Discuss rules about time. Talk about:

1. Your offices or other offices you know about

2. Your country or other countries you know about

B. People in the United States write dates differently than people in most other countries. They write dates in two ways:

May 27, 2004   <u>May</u>   <u>27</u> , <u>2004</u>
                Month   **Day**   **Year**

05/27/04   <u>05</u> / <u>27</u> / <u>04</u>
               Month **Day** **Year**

Change these dates to U.S. style (two ways).

Most Countries	The United States
1. 25 December 2003	December 25, 2003 or 12/25/03
2. 10 October 1931	
3. 19 March 1999	
4. 23 September 2006	
5. 30 April 2001	

EXPANSION

A. Design your own business card. Use the space below, or your own paper.

Example:

Andrea Noriega, Owner

Noriega Printing Services

1436 Frontier Avenue
Las Vegas, NV 89110

Phone: 702-684-3822
Fax: 702-684-3823
E-mail: Anoriega@lv.com

B. **Most people have to go to an interview before they get a job. Match the questions in *A* with the answers in *B*.**

A	**B**
____ 1. What is your work experience?	a. Here it is. It lists my jobs.
____ 2. How much education do you have?	b. Most recently, I worked in a restaurant.
____ 3. Do you know how to use a computer?	c. I know how to send e-mail and search online.
____ 4. Do you know how to use the Internet?	d. Yes, Microsoft Word.
____ 5. What hours can you work?	e. I'm taking some college classes.
____ 6. Do you have a résumé?	f. Afternoons and weekends.

OUR OWN STORIES

Tell your classmates about a time when you applied for a job. Or tell about something unusual that happened at work.

Clothing Customs

WHAT DO YOU THINK?

► Think about a country or culture you know well.
  Do people wear hats?

► Do they wear them indoors?

Hats Off

Read the story.

> I am a science professor. I teach at a university in the United States. Students call me Professor Singh. One day, my wife and I wanted to go out for dinner. We wanted to try a new restaurant.
>
> When we got to the restaurant, the manager asked me to take off my hat. I was angry. I told him it was not a hat and I could not remove it. The manager would not listen. He said that I had to remove my hat or he would not serve us food. My wife and I left the restaurant.

Can you guess?

Work in a small group. Answer these questions.

► The manager wanted Professor Singh to take off his hat. Why?

► Professor Singh refused to take off his hat. Why?

► Can you think of an explanation?

Let's find out.

Read the explanation.

Sikh—A person who practices the Sikh religion—a religion from India

turban—A long piece of cloth wrapped around the head

> In the United States, men take off their hats. This shows good manners. It is a sign of respect. The manager wanted his customers to use good manners in his restaurant. He felt that Professor Singh did not show him respect.
>
> Professor Singh is a Sikh from India. Sikh men must wear a turban at all times. Their turbans are symbols of pride. For a Sikh, removing his turban is disgraceful. Professor Singh wore his turban because of his religion. He would not take off his turban to eat in the restaurant.

Did the explanation surprise you? Why or why not?

COMPREHENSION

A. Read the story and the explanation again. Write _T_ (true) or _F_ (false).

___T___ 1. Professor Singh is a teacher.

_____ 2. The Singhs are from India.

_____ 3. The restaurant is in India.

_____ 4. The manager wanted Professor Singh to take off his turban.

_____ 5. Professor Singh was angry.

_____ 6. The Singhs did not eat at the restaurant.

B. Answer these questions with a partner.

1. Why did the manager want Professor Singh to remove his turban?
2. Why did Professor Singh refuse?

VOCABULARY

Rewrite the sentences. Use words from the box in place of the underlined words.

disgraceful	sign	indoors	~~manager~~	religion	remove

1. The <u>boss</u> did not understand Professor Singh's religious rules.

   The manager did not understand Professor Singh's religious rules.

2. Professor Singh followed the Sikh <u>set of beliefs</u>.

   _____

3. A Sikh's turban is a <u>symbol</u> of pride.

   _____

4. The manager wanted Professor Singh to <u>take off</u> his turban.

   _____

5. Sikhs must wear their turbans <u>inside restaurants</u>.

   _____

6. For Sikhs, not wearing a turban is <u>very bad and wrong</u>.

   _____

RETELL THE STORY

A. Work with a partner. Student A, retell Professor Singh's story. Student B, retell the explanation.

B. What do you think? Share your opinion with your partner.

1. Should restaurants have rules about their customers' clothing?

2. Imagine you are in the manager's situation. What do you do?

3. Imagine you are in Professor Singh's situation. What do you do?

DICTIONARY DISCOVERIES

In Unit 4, you learned that the same letters can have different sounds in different words. Also, different letters or groups of letters sometimes have the same sound. The dictionary tells you about this; for example, *I* and *eye* sound exactly the same, and the dictionary shows you this.

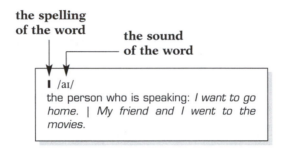

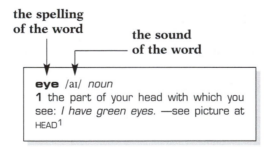

Look up these words in your dictionary. Write the sound of each word. Circle *same* or *different*. Practice saying the words with a partner.

1. a. won   /wʌn/   (same)/ different

    b. one   /wʌn/

2. a. not   _____   same / different

    b. knot   _____

3. a. off   _____   same / different

    b. of   _____

4. a. wear   _____   same / different

    b. where   _____

5. a. wear   _____   same / different

    b. were*   _____

* In some dictionaries, you may need to look up *be* to find *were*.

▲ CULTURE CAPSULE

A. Read the information.

Amish—Christians who follow strict religious rules, wear traditional clothes, and do not use things such as telephones, cars, or televisions

    In restaurants in the United States, everyone must wear shoes. In some restaurants, men have to wear jackets and ties. In many offices, on Fridays people dress more informally than they dress on other days. In these offices, Fridays are called "dress-down Fridays."

    Baseball caps are the most popular hats in the United States. Men, women, and children wear them. Besides the Sikhs, other groups have special hats. Some Jewish men wear small skullcaps. Amish men wear large, black felt hats.

B. Work in a small group. Discuss these questions.

1. What clothing rules do restaurants have?
2. What rules do business offices have?
3. Who wears baseball caps?
4. What men wear special hats?

A. Match the names of the hats in A with the pictures in B.

A

___e___ 1. hard hat

_____ 2. skullcap

_____ 3. baseball cap

_____ 4. top hat

_____ 5. sun hat

_____ 6. cowboy hat

B

a.

b.

c.

d.

e.

f.

B. Answer these questions in a small group. Talk about your culture or your family.

1. Do you remove your shoes indoors?

2. Can men have mustaches or beards? Do men have to have mustaches or beards?

3. Do you have rules about dress, pant, or sleeve length? For women? For men?

4. Are some colors only for women? Only for men?

5. Does clothing change when a child becomes an adult?

6. Do you have any "unisex" clothing that both men and women can wear?

EXPANSION

A. Draw a picture of clothing or jewelry from your family or culture. Write this information next to your drawing:

1. What do you call it?

2. What color is it?

3. Does it have a story?

4. Who wears it? When?

Example:

This is my green jade bracelet. My grandmother in China sent it to me when I was born. I wear it for birthdays, Chinese New Year, and weddings. When I have a daughter, I will give it to her.

B. Complete the crossword puzzle. Use the words in the box.

dress	pants	skirt	sweater
hat	shoes	socks	tie

Across

2.   3.   6.   7.

Down

1.   2.   4.   5.

❋ OUR OWN STORIES

Tell your classmates about an important occasion when you didn't like your clothes. What was the occasion? Why was it important? What was wrong with your clothes? Or tell about a time when your clothes were perfect.

Naming Customs

WHAT DO YOU THINK?

► Who gave you your name? Are you named after someone?

► Does your name mean something? What?

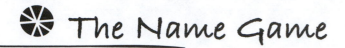

The Name Game

Read the story.

> My name is Melissa Gillis. I teach English in a high school in South Carolina. Roberto Vega is one of my students. In another class, I have a student named Alfredo Marino. They are both from El Salvador. Last month, the teachers had Parents' Night at the high school. I met Alfredo and Roberto's parents, Mr. and Mrs. Marino. The two boys have the same mother and father! They are brothers but have different last names.

Can you guess?

Work in a small group. Answer these questions.

► Roberto Vega and Alfredo Marino have different last names. Why?

► Is Roberto adopted? Are the boys trying to confuse Ms. Gillis?

► Can you think of any other explanation?

Let's find out.

Read the explanation.

Latin American countries— Countries in the Americas (like El Salvador) where they speak Spanish or Portuguese

> In many Latin American countries, people have two "last" (family) names. The first family name comes from the father. The second family name comes from the mother. The boys are actually Roberto Marino Vega and Alfredo Marino Vega. "Marino" comes from their father and "Vega" comes from their mother.
>
> When the boys started school in the United States, they wrote their names on a form. In the space for "last name," they wrote "Marino Vega." But in the United States, people are not used to double last names. A woman looked at Alfredo's form. She understood that Marino was his first family name, his father's name. She crossed out "Vega." From that day on, his last name for school was Marino. Another person looked at Roberto's form. This person decided that Roberto's last name was "Vega," and crossed out "Marino." Suddenly, the brothers had different last names!

Did the explanation surprise you? Why or why not?

COMPREHENSION

A. Read the story and the explanation again. Write the sentences in order.

~~Ms. Gillis found out that Alfredo and Roberto are brothers.~~

The boys' parents went to the high school for Parents' Night.

Someone crossed out "Vega," and someone else crossed out "Marino."

~~Roberto and Alfredo started school in the United States.~~

Ms. Gillis met Roberto and Alfredo's parents.

Alfredo and Roberto wrote "Marino Vega" on their school forms.

The brothers had different last names for school.

1. _Roberto and Alfredo started school in the United States._

2. _____

3. _____

4. _____

5. _____

6. _____

7. _Ms. Gillis found out that Alfredo and Roberto are brothers._

B. Answer these questions with a partner.

1. Why did the boys write two last names on their school forms?

2. Why did people at the school cross out names on the boys' forms?

VOCABULARY

Look at the story and the explanation. Match the words in _A_ with the meanings in _B_.

A	B
_c_ 1. Parents' Night	a. family name
___ 2. last name	b. really
___ 3. cross out	~~c. an evening when mothers and fathers talk with teachers~~
___ 4. be used to	d. a special paper for writing information
___ 5. double	e. two
___ 6. actually	f. choose
___ 7. form	g. after that
___ 8. from that day on	h. know about
___ 9. decide	i. make a line through

DICTIONARY DISCOVERIES

In Unit 12, you saw that words can have more than one meaning. The dictionary gives you all the meanings. When you look up a word, you have to choose the definition you need.

Here is what the dictionary says about the noun _name_. The first definition is the right one for the story "The Name Game."

---

name¹ /neɪm/ *noun*
1 the word that you call someone or something: *My name is Jane Smith.* | *What is the name of this town?*
2 someone who is famous: *She is a big name in fashion.*

Circle these words in "The Name Game." Look up each word in your dictionary. Write the definition that is right for the story. If there is an example sentence, write that too.

1. teach (verb)

_____

_____

2. form (noun)

_____

_____

3. space (noun)

_____

_____

RETELL THE STORY

A. Work with a partner. Student A, retell Ms. Gillis's story. Student B, retell the explanation.

B. What do you think? Share your opinion with your partner.

1. Imagine that you are in Roberto's or Alfredo's situation. Someone changes your name. How do you feel? What do you do?

2. Imagine that you are in Mr. and Mrs. Marino's situation. Someone changed your sons' names. How do you feel? What do you do?

3. Imagine that you are in Ms. Gillis's situation. You find out that someone changed your students' names. What do you do?

A. Read the information.

Some naming traditions are changing in the United States. Traditionally, when a woman got married, she stopped using her last name. She took her husband's last name. Today, some women do not change their names when they get married. They keep their maiden name (the original family name). Sometimes they keep their maiden name and add their husband's last name: Susan Stewart marries Alan Singer and becomes Susan Stewart-Singer. The husband sometimes changes his name too: Alan Singer becomes Alan Stewart-Singer. But not many men do this.

B. Answer these questions.

1. Traditionally, after Jennie Jarvis (a woman) married Wilbur Wilson, what was her last name?

   (one possibility) _____

2. Today, after Rory Stevens (a woman) marries Yale Cabot, what is her last name?

   (three possibilities) _____

   _____

✸ CULTURAL EXCHANGE

A. Answer these questions in a small group. Talk about your culture and other cultures you know about.

1. How many names does a person have?

2. Which names does a person have? Given name ("first name")? Another given name ("middle name")? Religious name? Family name ("last name")? Another family name? Something else?

3. Which name is first? Second? Third? Last?

4. Does the name change when someone gets married?

5. When a baby is born, what family name does the baby get?

6. Does a baby's given name come from a family member (is the baby "named after" a family member)?

B. **Interview a classmate. Ask these questions. Tell other classmates what you find out.**

1. Who chose your name? How did they choose it?

2. Does your name have a meaning? What is it?

3. Do you have a nickname (a short name that your family and friends call you)? What is it?

4. Were you named after someone? Do you look like that person? Do you act like that person?

EXPANSION

A. **These are popular first names for boys and girls in the United States. Unscramble the names.**

Girls' Names					
Abigail	Barbara	Brianne	~~Caitlin~~	Daniela	Melanie

1. tinacil   Caitlin
2. rarabba   _____
3. lagiaib   _____
4. nedalai   _____
5. eelmani   _____
6. naberin   _____

Boys' Names					
Brandon	~~Bradley~~	Charles	Matthew	Nicholas	Patrick

1. dabeylr   Bradley
2. whatmet   _____
3. criptka   _____
4. lanhcios   _____
5. drabnno   _____
6. seclhra   _____

B. A family tree is a drawing that shows how all the people in a family are related to each other. Make a family tree for your family or a friend's family. Tell a partner about the family tree. Show your partner . . .

you or your friend   brothers and sisters

grandparents   cousins

parents   children

aunts and uncles

- An equal sign (=) means that two people are married.
- Brothers and sisters (and their wives and husbands) go on the same line.
- Children go under their parents.

Example:

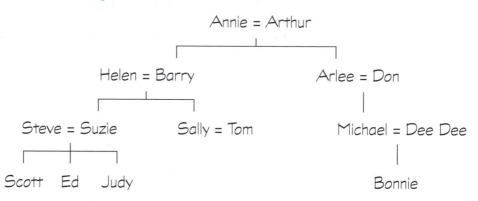

OUR OWN STORIES

Did anyone ever mispronounce your name or call you by the wrong name? Tell your classmates about it. Or tell about a time you made a mistake with another person's name.

The Hidden Meaning of Numbers

WHAT DO YOU THINK?

► What is your favorite number?

► Is there a number you don't like? What is it?

✳ Sorry, Wrong Number

Read the story.

> My name is Rod Sterling. I work for the telephone company in California. Last year, we had a problem. Many people bought cell phones, and we needed more telephone numbers. When many people need new phone numbers, we have to create a new area code. An area code is three numbers that come before a regular phone number. Everyone in the same geographic area has the same telephone area code.
>
> We changed part of area code 818 to 626. But some customers in that area were unhappy. They complained! They sent letters. They made phone calls. They called people in the state government. They even called the federal government in Washington, D.C.! We were stunned. We never thought people would object to the new area code.

Can you guess?

Work in a small group. Answer these questions.

► Customers objected to the new area code. Why?

► Did they just want to make trouble?

► Can you think of any other explanation?

Let's find out.

Read the explanation.

> The customers who complained were Chinese. They believe that the number 8 is lucky. Their old area code was 818. Two 8s in a phone number is extra lucky. It means prosperity.
>
> Changing to 626 was bad. Add 6, 2, and 6—the total is 14. Many Chinese people associate the number 4 with death. They do not want a phone number that means death. The Chinese customers wanted the telephone company to change 626 back to 818. But the customers did not succeed. They had to keep the new area code.

Did the explanation surprise you? Why or why not?

COMPREHENSION

A. Read the story and the explanation again. Write _T_ (true) or _F_ (false).

___F___ 1. Mr. Sterling does not work for the telephone company now.

_____ 2. His company needed more customers.

_____ 3. The old area code was 818. The new area code was 626.

_____ 4. All of the customers complained.

_____ 5. The people at the telephone company were surprised.

_____ 6. Some Chinese people believe that 818 is a lucky number.

_____ 7. Some Chinese people believe that 626 is an unlucky number.

_____ 8. The customers accepted the change quietly.

_____ 9. The telephone company changed the area code to 818 again.

B. Answer these questions with a partner.

1. Why did the telephone company need more phone numbers?

2. Who wanted the old area code, 818? Why?

3. Who didn't want the new area code, 626? Why?

VOCABULARY

What do the underlined words mean? Circle _a_ or _b_.

1. They had to <u>create</u> a new area code.

   (a.) make

   b. take away

2. They lived in the same <u>geographic area</u>.

   a. part of California

   b. house

3. Some <u>customers</u> were unhappy.

   a. people who worked for the company for a long time

   b. people who paid the company for their telephone service

4. They complained about the change.

   a. said they were unhappy with

   b. wrote letters to explain

5. We were stunned.

   a. happy

   b. surprised

6. They objected to the new area code.

   a. said they didn't like

   b. changed

7. Two 8s mean prosperity.

   a. sickness

   b. money

8. They associate the number 4 with death.

   a. think of

   b. add

9. The customers wanted to change the area code, but they did not succeed.

   a. make it happen

   b. talk about it

RETELL THE STORY

A. Work with a partner. Student A, retell Mr. Sterling's story. Student B, retell the explanation.

B. What do you think? Share your opinion with your partner.

1. Some Chinese customers did not like the new area code. They complained. Were they right?

2. The phone company did not change the new area code. Were they right?

3. Is it good to complain to a company when you don't like something?

DICTIONARY DISCOVERIES

For pronunciation, words are divided into syllables, or sound parts. In the last sentence, *for* has one syllable, *into* has two syllables, and *divided* has three syllables. The dictionary shows how many syllables a word has. It puts a small mark between the syllables. *Customer* has three syllables— three parts when you say it.

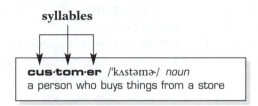

Look up these words in your dictionary. Put a mark between the syllables. Write the number of syllables.

1. g o v/e r n/m e n t   3
2. c o d e   1
3. a r e a   _____
4. p r o s p e r i t y   _____
5. a s s o c i a t e   _____
6. c r e a t e   _____
7. e i g h t   _____

A. Read the information.

In the United States, the number 13 is unlucky. Friday the 13th is the most unlucky day. Most hotels do not have a 13th floor—the floor above 12 is 14. In some cities with numbered streets, there is no 13th Street. Instead, they give the street a name. In Santa Monica, California, 13th Street is called Euclid Street.

Some wedding anniversaries are special. A couple's 25th wedding anniversary is called the Silver Anniversary. Friends and family give the couple gifts of silver. The 50th anniversary is called the Golden Anniversary, and people give gifts of gold.

Numbers are important in many games. "Twenty-one" is the name of a popular card game. The numbers 7 and 11 are considered lucky numbers. These are winning numbers in many games. Millions of people buy tickets with lucky numbers on them. Then the people watch for "their" numbers on TV. If the numbers on TV are the same as the numbers on a person's ticket, that person can win millions of dollars.

B. Discuss these questions with a partner.

1. Why is there no 13th Street in Santa Monica, California?

2. When do people give gold? When do they give silver?

3. What are some lucky gambling numbers?

✱ CULTURAL EXCHANGE

A. What do you know about numbers in different cultures? Do you know about the following customs? Do you know about other customs or beliefs about numbers? Work with a group and share what you know.

- Armenians usually give uneven numbers of flowers (one, three, five, and so on). But when someone dies, they give an even number of flowers (two, four, six, and so on).

- For weddings, most Japanese people give uneven numbers of things as gifts (for example, plates or cups). It is too easy to divide even numbers of things between the wife and the husband if they divorce. Everyone wants the couple to stay together.

- In England, people used to believe that the seventh child in a family could see the future.

- Some Jewish people believe that 18 means life. They often give eighteen dollars to babies.

B. Read the rhyme. In the United States, some children learn numbers with this rhyme. Did you or your children learn numbers with a rhyme or song? Say it or sing it for your classmates.

One, two, buckle my shoe.
Three, four, shut the door.
Five, six, pick up sticks.
Seven, eight, lay them straight.
Nine, ten, let's say it again.

EXPANSION

A. Change the numbers to letters and find a message. 1 = A, 2 = B, and so on.

1	2	3	4	5	6	7	8	9	10	11	12	13	14	15	16	17	18	19	20	21	22	23	24	25	26
A	B	C	D	E	F	G	H	I	J	K	L	M	N	O	P	Q	R	S	T	U	V	W	X	Y	Z

```
___  ___  ___  ___  ___  ___  ___      ___  ___  ___
14   21   13    2    5   18   19        3    1   14

___  ___      ___  ___  ___ .
 2    5        6   21   14
```

B. What was a good year in your life? Write it down. Then write the reasons it was good for you. Tell a partner about your good year.

_____ was a very good year for me.
(year)

1. _____

2. _____

3. _____

4. _____

5. _____

OUR OWN STORIES

Do you have a lucky number? Tell your classmates about it. Or tell about a time a number was important in your life.

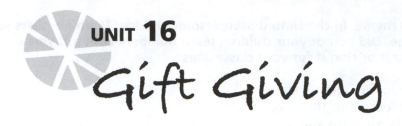

UNIT 16
Gift Giving

WHAT DO YOU THINK?

► Did you ever give a person a gift that he or she did not like?

► Did you ever pretend to like a gift that someone gave you?

 **If the Shoe Fits**

Read the story.

> My name is Ray Dryden. I work in a big shoe store in Boston. One day, a woman came into the store with her son. He was about twelve years old and he was looking for shoes. He tried on many different pairs. Finally, he chose a pair of sneakers.
>
> I told the mother the price. Then she walked away from me. She stopped another customer and asked her something. Then the boy's mother gave the other customer some money. The other woman came over to me and paid for the shoes. I don't think the two women knew each other. It was very strange.

sneakers—Sports shoes

Can you guess?

Work in a small group. Answer these questions.

► The boy's mother did not give the money to Mr. Dryden. Why not? Was she afraid of him?

► Can you think of any other explanation?

Let's find out.

Read the explanation.

> The boy, Paulino, and his mother are from the Cape Verde Islands. These islands are in the Atlantic Ocean near the west coast of Africa. Cape Verdeans have a belief about shoes. If you give shoes to someone you love, that person will leave you. Paulino's mother loved her son. She did not want him to leave her. That is why she asked the other customer to pay for the shoes. The shoes were not a gift from Paulino's mother, so she would not lose her son.

Did the explanation surprise you? Why or why not?

COMPREHENSION

A. Read the story and the explanation again. Write _T_ (true) or _F_ (false).

_T_ 1. Ray Dryden sells shoes.

____ 2. The boy wanted some shoes.

____ 3. The boy took a long time to find the right shoes.

____ 4. The other customer was a friend.

____ 5. The boy's name is Paulino.

____ 6. The boy and his mother are from Boston.

____ 7. The boy wanted to leave his mother.

____ 8. The mother didn't have enough money.

B. Answer these questions in a small group.

1. What did Paulino's mother believe about shoes?

2. What did the other customer do for Paulino's mother? Why?

VOCABULARY

What do the underlined words mean? Circle _a_ or _b_.

1. Paulino <u>tried on</u> many shoes.

    a. asked his mother for

    (b.) put his feet into

2. She <u>stopped</u> another customer.

    a. said, "Excuse me," and asked a question

    b. said, "Goodbye," and walked away

3. The women did not know <u>each other</u>.

    a. Paulino's mother and the other woman

    b. Paulino's mother and everyone in the United States

4. It was very <u>strange</u>.

    a. surprising

    b. not surprising

5. The islands are near the <u>west coast</u> of Africa.

    a. the side where the sun comes up

    b. the side where the sun goes down

6. They have a <u>belief</u> about shoes.

    a. an idea

    b. a gift

7. His mother did not want the shoes to be a <u>gift</u> from her.

    a. something you give or receive

    b. something you say or do

DICTIONARY DISCOVERIES

Circle these words in "If the Shoe Fits." Look up each word in your dictionary. Write the definition that is right for the story. If there is an example sentence, write that too.

1. about

    _____

    _____

2. stopped (Look up *stop*.)

    _____

    _____

3. each other (Look up *each*.)

    _____

    _____

4. belief

    _____

    _____

RETELL THE STORY

A. Work with a partner. Student A, retell Mr. Dryden's story. Student B, retell the explanation.

B. What do you think? Share your opinion with your partner.

1. Imagine that you are in Mr. Dryden's situation. Your customer will not give you the money herself. What do you think? What do you do?

2. Imagine that you are in Paulino's situation. Your mother will not give Mr. Dryden the money herself. How do you feel? What do you say?

3. Imagine that you are shopping. Someone gives you money and asks you to pay for something. What do you think? What do you do?

▲ CULTURE CAPSULE

Christmas—A Christian holiday

Hanukkah—A Jewish holiday

Kwanza—An African-American holiday

A. Read the information.

In the United States, people give gifts for birthdays, high school or college graduations, weddings, and wedding anniversaries. People also give gifts to friends who have had a baby or who have moved into a new home. Most people give gifts for Christmas, Hanukkah, or Kwanza. And it is a custom to bring a small gift when you eat or stay at someone's home. If someone gives you a gift, you open it immediately and thank the person. If you receive a gift by mail, you call or write very soon after receiving it to say thank you.

B. Discuss these questions with a partner.

1. What are three holidays when Americans give gifts?
2. Name some other times Americans give gifts.

✿ CULTURAL EXCHANGE

A. When do people give gifts? Answer for you, your culture, and other cultures you know about. Work with a group and share what you know.

Who	Give Gifts For . . .
1. African-Americans	Kwanza, Christmas, graduations, weddings, birthdays, anniversaries, new homes, new babies
2.	
3.	
4.	
5.	

B. Read these gift-giving customs from other cultures. What other gift-giving customs do you know about? Work with a group and share what you know.

- In Japan, people never wrap presents in white. White is for death.
- In Hawaii, grandmothers make special blankets for new grandbabies.
- When Korean babies are 100 days old, family members and close friends give gifts of gold.
- Chinese people do not give gifts of knives, scissors, or umbrellas. These things mean the friendship will end.
- When a Korean man turns sixty, his family and his close friends give him money in a double envelope.

Gift Giving **117**

EXPANSION

A. Choose three gifts for yourself—anything in the world! Write them below. Why did you choose them? Explain your choices to a partner.

1. _____

2. _____

3. _____

B. How do people say thank you? Match the words in *A* with the languages and countries in *B*. Then add more thank yous, languages, and countries that you know.

A	B
_e_ 1. thank you	a. Italian / Italy
___ 2. merci	b. Korean / Korea
___ 3. grazie	c. Russian / Russia
___ 4. arigato	d. Japanese / Japan
___ 5. gracias	~~e. English / Australia~~
___ 6. spasibo	f. Portuguese / Brazil
___ 7. obrigado	g. French / Canada
___ 8. kamsa hamnida	h. Spanish / Mexico
___ 9. _____	i. _____
___ 10. _____	j. _____
___ 11. _____	k. _____
___ 12. _____	l. _____

OUR OWN STORIES

Tell your classmates about a time when you received a special or surprising gift. Or tell about a time when you gave someone a special gift.

UNIT 17
Gender

WHAT DO YOU THINK?

► Do you touch people in public? Do you touch men or women, or both?

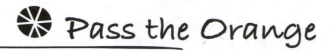

Pass the Orange

Read the story.

My name is Jan Riley. I find American homes for international students to live in while they go to college in the United States. One time, I had students from Korea, Taiwan, and Japan. I planned a picnic for them on Independence Day, the Fourth of July.

We went to a park and ate hot dogs, hamburgers, and watermelon. Later, I taught them a game called "pass the orange."

The students sat in a circle on the ground. They sat in this order: boy, girl, boy, girl, and so on. A boy had to hold an orange under his chin and put it under the chin of the girl next to him. Then the girl had to put the orange under the chin of the boy on her other side. They could not use their hands. If a boy and girl dropped the orange, they were out of the game.

The students kept dropping the orange quickly. But they laughed a lot, so I thought that the game was fun for them. They played the game several times. A few days later, I heard that some of the students complained about the game.

Can you guess?

Work in a small group. Answer these questions.

► The students didn't like the game called "pass the orange." Why not? Did they think the game was for children?

► Can you think of any other explanation?

Let's find out.

Read the explanation.

The students were from countries where traditionally men and women don't touch each other in public. When the students passed the orange, they had to be very close to each other. Their faces had to touch. This made them uncomfortable. They laughed but they did not think the game was fun. The students were embarrassed. The game broke their cultures' rules.

Did the explanation surprise you? Why or why not?

COMPREHENSION

A. Read the story and the explanation again. Write *T* (true) or *F* (false).

__F__ 1. The students were in high school.

_____ 2. The students were from North America.

_____ 3. It was a holiday.

_____ 4. They ate in a park.

_____ 5. In the game, girls sat next to girls, and boys sat next to boys.

_____ 6. The students had to eat an orange together.

_____ 7. The students liked the game.

_____ 8. Mrs. Riley thought the students liked the game.

B. Answer these questions with a partner.

1. Mrs. Riley wanted to do something nice for the students. Did she succeed?

2. Why did the students laugh? Why did they complain?

3. The game broke the students' cultural rules. What rules? How did it break them?

VOCABULARY

Look at the story and the explanation. Write *S* if the words below are similar. Write *D* if they are different.

__S__ 1. picnic / meal outside

_____ 2. chin / hand

_____ 3. kept dropping / dropped many times

_____ 4. traditionally / by custom

_____ 5. in public / when people can see them

_____ 6. passed / did not give

_____ 7. embarrassed / uncomfortable

_____ 8. broke / respected

DICTIONARY DISCOVERIES

Circle these words in "Pass the Orange." Look up each word in your dictionary. Write the definition that is right for the story. If there is an example sentence, write that too.

1. hold (verb)

   _____

   _____

2. game (noun)

   _____

   _____

3. ground (noun)

   _____

   _____

4. dropped (Look up *drop*, verb)

   _____

   _____

RETELL THE STORY

A. Work with a partner. Student A, retell Mrs. Riley's story. Student B, retell the explanation.

B. What do you think? Share your opinion with your partner.

1. Mrs. Riley chose the wrong game for these students. Why?

2. The students didn't tell Mrs. Riley that they were embarrassed. They complained later. Why?

3. Imagine that you are playing pass the orange with the students. How do you feel? What do you do?

4. Imagine that you are planning a picnic for the same students. Will you play games? What games?

A. Read the information.

In the United States, boys and girls go to the same public schools and have classes together. Boys and girls can touch each other on their faces and arms. At any age, males and females can touch each other while they are dancing. Unmarried men and women can be alone together.

Men and women also work together in the United States. Today, more women are becoming lawyers, doctors, pilots, police officers, firefighters, and military personnel. More men are becoming flight attendants, nurses, kindergarten teachers, and secretaries. Some women are heads of corporations and universities. Some women have high positions in government. But many more men than women still hold these jobs.

B. Read these sentences about the United States. Write _T_ (true) or _F_ (false).

___T___ 1. Boys and girls go to school together.

_____ 2. Boys and girls never touch each other.

_____ 3. Males and females cannot touch each other while dancing.

_____ 4. Unmarried men and women cannot be alone together.

_____ 5. More women have jobs that only men had before.

_____ 6. More men have jobs that only women had before.

_____ 7. Men have most high-level jobs.

❋ CULTURAL EXCHANGE

A. Answer these questions in a small group. Talk about your culture or your family.

1. Who gets more attention, baby boys or baby girls?

2. Can boys play with dolls? Can girls play with toy trucks?

3. Do girls and boys get the same education?

4. Do they go to school together?

5. Can unmarried men and women dance together?

6. Can unmarried men and women be alone together?

7. Are some jobs for women only? What jobs?

8. Are some jobs for men only? What jobs?

B. Give three reasons why it's good to be a female in your family or culture. Give three reasons why it's good to be a male. Discuss your answers with a group.

Why it's good to be a female . . .

1. _____

2. _____

3. _____

Why it's good to be a male . . .

1. _____

2. _____

3. _____

 EXPANSION

A. Complete the crossword puzzle. Use words in the story "Pass the Orange."

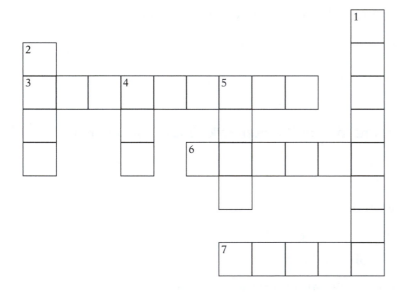

Across

3.

6.

7.

Down

1.

2.

4.

5.

B. You are making plans to do some things with family members. You will do things with different family members at different times. Will you make the same plans for males and females of the same age? Discuss your plans with a partner.

Where will you go? What will you do with . . .

1. your twelve-year-old niece?

_____

_____

2. your twelve-year-old nephew?

_____

_____

3. your grandmother?

_____

_____

4. your grandfather?

_____

_____

5. your sister?

_____

_____

6. your brother?

_____

_____

✹ OUR OWN STORIES

Did you ever have a problem in school or at work because you were a male or a female? What was it? Tell your classmates. Or tell about how women and men show respect to each other in your culture.

UNIT 18

Religious Customs

WHAT DO YOU THINK?

► Do you have any religious beliefs or customs?

► What do you know about different religions?

✺ My Brother's Keeper

Read the story.

> My name is Fay, and I live in New York City. One Friday last January, I had a strange experience. It was late when I left work. It was very cold. I walked from the bus to my apartment and saw my new neighbor, Shoshana. She was standing outside our apartment building. She stopped a woman and asked her something. The woman looked at Shoshana, shook her head, and walked away. Shoshana stopped the next person, a man. He nodded and followed her inside the building. I was worried, so I went to her apartment and knocked on her door.
>
> "Shoshana, it's me, Fay. Is everything all right?"
>
> Shoshana came to the door and invited me in. The man from the street stood next to Shoshana's electric heater. He turned it on.

Can you guess?

Work in a small group. Answer these questions.

▶ The man turned on Shoshana's heater. Why?

▶ Didn't Shoshana know how to do it?

▶ Can you think of any other explanation?

Let's find out.

Read the explanation.

Sabbath—A religious day of rest for Jews and some Christians

non-Jew—A person who is not Jewish

> Shoshana is an Orthodox Jew. Her religion says that she cannot do any work on the Sabbath. The rule is very strict. She cannot even turn things on and off. But it is all right if a non-Jew does it for her.
>
> The Sabbath begins at sunset on Friday. Shoshana got home too late to turn on the heater before sunset. It was very cold. That is why she stopped people on the street. The man who stopped was not Jewish. He often helped his Jewish neighbors. He turned off air conditioners, lights, and stoves for them. He was happy to help his Jewish neighbors on their Sabbath.

Did the explanation surprise you? Why or why not?

COMPREHENSION

A. Read the story and the explanation again. Write _F_ (Fay), _S_ (Shoshana), or _B_ (both).

_B_ 1. She lives in New York City.

____ 2. She got home late.

____ 3. She talked to people on the street.

____ 4. She could not turn on her heater.

____ 5. She was worried.

____ 6. She went to the other woman's apartment.

____ 7. A man helped her.

B. Answer these questions with a partner.

1. What is the Jewish rule about working on the Sabbath?

2. What was Shoshana's problem that Friday?

3. How did she solve her problem?

4. Why was it all right for the man to help her?

VOCABULARY

Look at the story and the explanation. Match the words in _A_ with the explanations in _B_.

A	B
_g_ 1. neighbor	a. something that happens to you or something that you do
____ 2. shook her head	b. walked behind
____ 3. experience	c. a machine that makes a place warm
____ 4. nodded	d. turned it left and right
____ 5. sunset	e. made a sound on the door
____ 6. heater	f. something that has many small places to live inside
____ 7. knocked	g. someone who lives near you
____ 8. followed	h. the end of the day
____ 9. apartment building	i. made it start and stop
____ 10. turned (it) on and off	j. moved his head up and down

A. Work with a partner. Student A, retell Fay's story. Student B, retell the explanation.

B. What do you think? Share your opinion with your partner.

1. Were Fay and Shoshana close friends?

2. Shoshana invited a man into her apartment. She didn't know the man. Was this a good idea?

3. Imagine that Shoshana stops you on the street. She asks you to turn on her heater. What do you think? What do you do?

4. In Orthodox Jewish neighborhoods, there is often a non-Jew who helps on the Sabbath. Does this surprise you? (Elvis Presley, the "King of Rock 'n' Roll," did this as a teenager.)

DICTIONARY DISCOVERIES

The dictionary tells you the sounds and the syllables of a word. It also tells you which syllable is louder than the others. A special mark comes before the loud syllable. It is called a "stress mark," and the loud sound is called "stress."

> **neigh·bor** /ˈneɪbə/ *noun*
> **1** someone who lives near you: *He is my* **next-door** *neighbor.*
> **2** someone who is sitting next to you: *Don't copy the answers from your neighbor's paper.*

Neighbor has two syllables. The stress mark is before the first syllable. The word sounds like this: NEIGH bor.

Look up these words in your dictionary. Mark between the syllables. Then underline the stressed syllable. Practice saying the words with a partner.

1. <u>n e i g h</u>/b o r
2. e x p e r i e n c e
3. i n s i d e (adverb)
4. a p a r t m e n t
5. b u i l d i n g
6. i n v i t e

A. Read the information.

Buddhists, Christians, Hindus, Jews, and Muslims live in the United States. There are also many smaller religious groups. There is no national religion. About 50 percent of Americans say they are religious, but many go to services only on special religious holidays. About 43 percent of Americans say they are not religious. In some parts of the country (especially the South), religion is a big part of social and community life. In other areas, it is not as important.

People of different religions often work together. Sometimes two religious groups have services together for a special occasion. There is a tradition of outdoor religious displays in December. One year, in California, there were three displays near each other on the same street. The Muslims had a Ramadan display, the Christians had a Christmas display, and the Jews had a Hanukkah display.

services—
Religious meetings

social—With other people

community—All of the city or town

displays—
Something for people to look at

B. Read these sentences about the United States. Write *T* (true) or *F* (false).

_F_ 1. Christianity is the national religion.

_____ 2. Half of Americans say they are religious.

_____ 3. Religion is more important in the South.

_____ 4. Ramadan is a Muslim holiday.

❋ CULTURAL EXCHANGE

A. Answer these questions in a small group. Talk about your neighborhood, your community, and your country.

1. What religions are there? Which is the biggest?

2. Does your country have a national religion?

3. Does religion have a big part in social life? In community life?

4. Are most people religious?

5. Do people go to services every day? Every week? Only on special religious holidays?

6. Is there more than one religion? Do people from different religions ever do special things together?

B. Answer these questions in a small group. Talk about your religion or other religions you know about.

1. What do people call their religious leaders?

2. Do the religious leaders wear special clothing? What do they wear?

3. What do people call their religious buildings?

4. What do they call their religious book(s)?

5. What are the most important religious holidays?

6. Is there a special day each week for the religion? What day is it? What is it called?

 EXPANSION

A. Find these words in the word square. Circle the words.

BUS	FAY	~~SHOSHANA~~	NEIGHBOR
SABBATH	HEATER	MAN	SUNSET

The words go four ways: right → left ← down ↓ up ↑

```
S   H   O   S   H   A   N   A
A   K   L   T   E   Z   R   R
B   U   S   E   A   F   O   C
B   N   H   S   T   K   Y   J
A   A   E   N   E   C   A   C
T   M   F   U   R   M   F   B
H   G   L   S   C   T   M   A
N   E   I   G   H   B   O   R
```

B. Write a holiday greeting to a friend of a different religion than yours. Write your friend's name in the first space. Write your name in the last space. Complete the message with words from the list, or use your own words.

I	**Happy Birthday of the Buddha**	time
we		holiday
my family and I	**Merry Christmas**	
	Happy Diwali	
	Happy Hanukkah	
	Blessed Ramadan	
Muslims	**family**	**Love,**
Jews	**children**	**Affectionately,**
Buddhists	**loved ones**	**All the best,**
Christians	**friends**	**Sincerely,**
Hindus		

Dear _____ ,
(person's name)

_____ want to wish you a very

_____ . I know this is an important

_____ for _____ .

I hope you are spending it with your _____ .

_____

_____
(your name)

✦ OUR OWN STORIES

Tell your classmates about a religious service that you remember. Where were you? What was the occasion? Why do you remember it?

UNIT 19
Age

WHAT DO YOU THINK?

► Is there an older person you respect very much? Who is it? Why do you respect that person?

► Is there an older person you do not like? Why don't you like that person?

Age Cannot Hide

Read the story.

> My name is Patchara. Fifteen years ago, I moved to the United States from Thailand. I work as a waitress in a restaurant. An older man and woman come in for dinner once a week. They are very nice. When they enter, I say, "Hello, Papa. Hello, Mama." Then I put my hands together and bow. That is how we greet older people in Thailand. It shows respect. But this couple doesn't like it. Now, when they come in, they don't want to sit in my area. They want a different waitress to serve them.

Can you guess?

Work in a small group. Answer these questions.

► The man and woman don't want Patchara to be their waitress. Why not?

► Is Patchara a bad waitress?

► Can you think of any other explanation?

Let's find out.

Read the explanation.

> Patchara embarrassed the couple. She drew attention to their age. These customers feel young. They don't want to think they look old. In fact, they are not young. Last year, their children gave them a party to celebrate their fiftieth wedding anniversary. They are proud of their long marriage and proud of their grandchildren, but they don't want to think about their age. Many Americans are not happy to get old.

Did the explanation surprise you? Why or why not?

COMPREHENSION

A. Read the story and the explanation again. Write *T* (true) or *F* (false).

__T__ 1. Patchara was born in Asia.

____ 2. She lives in the United States now.

____ 3. She works in a restaurant.

____ 4. A man and woman eat dinner at the restaurant once a month.

____ 5. The man and woman are the same age as Patchara.

____ 6. Patchara does not like them.

____ 7. Their wedding was more than sixty years ago.

____ 8. They don't have any grandchildren.

B. Answer these questions with a partner.

1. How does Patchara greet the couple? Why does she do this?

2. How do the man and woman feel when Patchara greets them? Why do they feel this way?

3. What is the situation now?

VOCABULARY

Look at the story and the explanation. Match the words in *A* with the meanings in *B*.

A	B
__h__ 1. waitress	a. where my tables are
____ 2. bow	b. happy about
____ 3. couple	c. really, actually
____ 4. in my area	d. made people think about
____ 5. serve	e. lean your body forward to show respect
____ 6. drew attention to	f. a celebration for people who are married for fifty years
____ 7. in fact	g. bring food to
____ 8. fiftieth wedding anniversary	h. a woman who brings food in a restaurant
____ 9. proud	i. a man and woman together

Age **135**

DICTIONARY DISCOVERIES

Circle these words in "Age Cannot Hide." Look up each word in your dictionary. Write the definition that is right for the story. If there is an example sentence, write that too.

1. bow (verb)

   _____

   _____

2. attention

   _____

   _____

3. anniversary

   _____

   _____

4. proud

   _____

   _____

RETELL THE STORY

A. Work with a partner. Student A, retell Patchara's story. Student B, retell the explanation.

B. What do you think? Share your opinion with your partner.

1. Should Patchara continue to bow to this couple? Should she continue to call them "Mama" and "Papa"?

2. Should the restaurant manager tell Patchara to say "Good evening" and not bow? Why or why not?

3. Should Patchara apologize to the couple? Why or why not?

4. Imagine that you are in the couple's situation. You are old, and Patchara is drawing attention to your age. How do you feel? What do you do?

A. Read the information.

In the United States, people over sixty-five are called "senior citizens." Sixty-five is the usual age to retire from work. After age sixty-five, most people receive some money from the government every month. Most senior citizens also get help from the government to pay for health care. And many younger workers save money for retirement. Senior citizens usually pay less than other people to ride buses and airplanes. They also pay less to see movies. And sometimes senior citizens pay less in restaurants and stores.

Some senior citizens live independently or with family members. Others live in retirement communities with other older people. There, they play sports and games. They take art and computer classes. They also have many social activities, such as concerts and dances. Young people are not allowed to live in retirement communities.

B. Work in a small group. Discuss these questions.

1. At what age do most Americans stop working?

2. How do they pay for things after they stop working?

3. Where do senior citizens live? Give three answers.

4. How do people spend their time in retirement communities?

CULTURAL EXCHANGE

Answer these questions in a small group. Talk about people in your family, community, and culture and other cultures you know about.

1. At what age do people retire?

2. How do they pay for things after they retire?

3. Where do they live?

4. How do they spend their time after they retire?

5. Are there any special rules to help older people? What are they?

A. Look at the example. Then make your own lifeline. Mark at least three important ages in your life and write what happened at those ages. Then find a partner and talk about your lifelines.

Example:

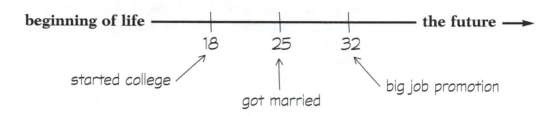

Your lifeline:

beginning of life —————————————————— **the future** ⟶

B. A couple in another country wants to know about the lives of older people in your country. Write them a letter. Begin your letter like this:

Dear Mr. and Mrs. _____,

I am from _____. In my country, older people . . .

OUR OWN STORIES

Tell your classmates a story about one of your grandparents. Or tell about another older person who is important to you.

UNIT 20

Healing

WHAT DO YOU THINK?

► When you have a health problem, who do you go to? A doctor? Someone else?

Banki

Read the story.

> I came to the United States from Russia about four years ago. I couldn't speak English. I had a bad cough, so I went to the hospital. The nurse came out and called my name, "Sergei Karpov." She asked me some questions, but I couldn't understand her.
>
> She took me to a small room, and I met the doctor. He listened to my chest. Then he saw my back. He pointed to my back and said something. I didn't understand his English, but I knew what he meant. He wanted to know about the red circles on my back. I said, *"Banki,"* but he didn't understand. The doctor shook his head. He looked upset.

Can you guess?

Work in a small group. Answer these questions.

► Sergei had red circles on his back. Why?

► Did he have a skin problem?

► Can you think of any other explanation?

Let's find out.

Read the explanation.

banki cup

pneumonia—A serious sickness in the chest

antibiotics— Medicine to fight bacteria

> The doctor called in a translator. The translator spoke Russian and English. She explained the circles on Sergei's back. The circles came from ten special glass cups, called *banki*. Russians use banki to treat bad chest colds and coughs.
>
> Sergei's mother used these cups on his back. She heated the banki and placed them upside down on Sergei's back. She left the cups on his skin for five minutes. The cups cooled. This made extra blood come into Sergei's skin. Under the cups, Sergei's skin became red. Then Sergei's mother gently removed the banki.
>
> Sergei went to bed. Usually, he felt better after his mother used banki to treat him. This time Sergei did not get better. He had pneumonia. He went to the hospital. The doctor gave Sergei antibiotics, and he got well.

Did the explanation surprise you? Why or why not?

COMPREHENSION

A. Read the story and the explanation again. Write *T* (true) or *F* (false).

_T_ 1. Sergei is from Russia.

____ 2. Sergei couldn't speak English.

____ 3. The doctor saw red marks on Sergei's back.

____ 4. The doctor knew about banki.

____ 5. Sergei explained banki to the doctor.

____ 6. The doctor put banki on Sergei's back.

____ 7. The banki made Sergei feel better.

____ 8. Sergei had a cold.

B. Answer these questions in a small group.

1. What do Russians use banki for?

2. Why did Sergei go to the hospital?

3. Why was the doctor upset?

4. What helped Sergei get well?

VOCABULARY

What do the underlined words mean? Circle *a* or *b*.

1. The <u>nurse</u> asked him some questions.

    a. doctor

    b. doctor's helper

2. The doctor called in a <u>translator</u>.

    a. person who spoke both languages

    b. person who knew Sergei

3. Sergei's mother used <u>banki</u> on his back.

    a. glass cups

    b. red circles

4. Russians use banki to <u>treat colds</u>.

    a. study colds

    b. make colds get better

Healing **141**

5. His mother <u>heated</u> the cups.

    a. explained

    b. made warm

6. She placed the banki <u>upside down</u> on his back.

    a. with the tops on his back

    b. with the bottoms on his back

7. Extra <u>blood</u> came into Sergei's skin.

    a. red liquid in the body

    b. brown marks on the body

8. Banki leave red circles on the <u>skin</u>.

    a. the inside of the body

    b. the outside of the body

9. This time Sergei did not <u>get better</u>.

    a. become well

    b. go to the doctor

DICTIONARY DISCOVERIES

Circle these words in "Banki." Look up each word in your dictionary. Write the definition. If there is an example sentence, write that too.

1. cough (noun)

    _____

    _____

2. chest

    _____

    _____

3. colds (Look up _cold_, noun)

    _____

    _____

4. back (noun)

    _____

    _____

RETELL THE STORY

A. Work with a partner. Student A, retell Sergei's story. Student B, retell the explanation.

B. What do you think? Share your opinion with your partner.

1. Imagine that you are in Sergei's situation. You are at the hospital, you are sick, and nobody understands you. How do you feel? What do you do?

2. Imagine that you are in the doctor's situation. You see red circles on someone's back. What do you think?

3. What do you think of Sergei's mother? Was it right to try the banki? Why or why not?

▲ CULTURE CAPSULE

A. Read the information.

In the United States, most people try to treat coughs and colds at home. They drink chicken soup, special teas, or a lot of water. They may take a lot of vitamin C. If people do not get better, they go to the doctor. Sometimes they have the flu, and doctors do not want to give them antibiotics. Doctors know that antibiotics cannot help the flu. But sometimes people want antibiotics. And sometimes doctors give antibiotics to people who have the flu.

Americans also do other things for their health. For example, traditional Chinese medicine is becoming popular. People use medicines made from special plants. People go to healers who are not doctors. People also take yoga classes. They want their bodies and their minds to work together for good health.

B. Discuss these questions with a partner.

1. For coughs and colds, what four things do Americans do before they go to a doctor?

2. Do antibiotics help the flu?

3. What kind of medicine is becoming popular in the United States?

4. What are some things Americans do for good health?

✸ CULTURAL EXCHANGE

A. Answer these questions in a small group. Talk about yourself, your family, and your culture.

1. What do you do for a cough or a cold? Does it help?

2. How often do you go to the doctor? Once a year? Twice a year? More? Less?

3. Who else treats you when you are sick? Your mother? A healer (not a doctor)?

4. Did you ever take an antibiotic for a cold or the flu? Did you get it from a doctor? Do you think it helped?

B. Interview three people. What things do most people do to stay well? Fill in the chart. Share the information with your class.

What Do You Do to Stay Well?

	Example	Person 1	Person 2	Person 3
Eat	garlic			
Drink	tea			
Wear	copper bracelet			
Do	swimming			

✸ EXPANSION

A. Read the saying. What does it mean? Is it only about apples? Is it only about food? Do you know any sayings in another language about staying healthy? Work with a group and share your ideas.

An apple a day keeps the doctor away.

B. Imagine you have a sick child. Your child cannot go to school. Write a note to the teacher. Follow the example.

Example:

Dear Mrs. Richards,

My daughter, Judy, will not be in school today or tomorrow.

She has a bad cold. Please give her homework to her brother.

Thank you,

Jeff Brown 626-555-0362

Brownie22@aoa.com

Your note:

OUR OWN STORIES

Tell your classmates about a time when someone was sick. Who was it? What was wrong? Who helped? How did they help?

World Map

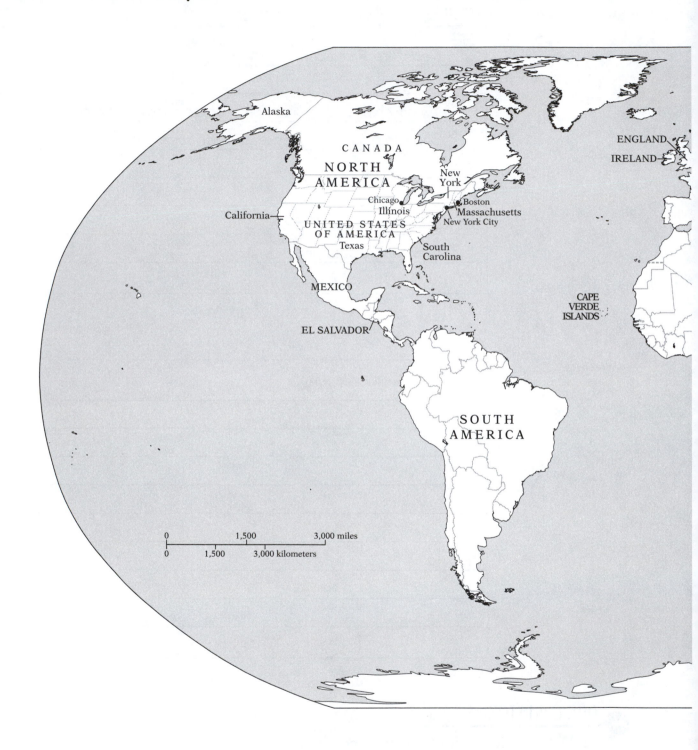

Alaska

CANADA

NORTH AMERICA

New York

Chicago
Illinois

Boston
Massachusetts
New York City

California

UNITED STATES OF AMERICA

Texas

South Carolina

MEXICO

EL SALVADOR

SOUTH AMERICA

ENGLAND

IRELAND

CAPE VERDE ISLANDS

0   1,500   3,000 miles
0   1,500   3,000 kilometers

DENMARK

RUSSIA

London

EUROPE

ARMENIA

ASIA

NORTH
KOREA

JAPAN

Tokyo

CHINA

IRAN

SOUTH
KOREA

KUWAIT

TAIWAN

AFRICA

INDIA

THAILAND

FEDERATED STATES
OF MICRONESIA

ETHIOPIA

CAMBODIA

Pohnpei

AUSTRALIA

NEW
ZEALAND

ANTARCTICA

Answer Key

UNIT 1

Comprehension A
2. F   4. F   6. T
3. F   5. T

Vocabulary
2. b   4. a   6. a
3. a   5. b   7. b

Dictionary Discoveries A
2. behave   8. scold
3. celebrate   9. seventh
4. finally   10. show
5. luck   11. stop
6. scold   12. student

Dictionary Discoveries B
(Answers will vary between dictionaries.)

UNIT 2

Comprehension A
2. Jon saw the couple with the baby.
3. Jon pointed to the couple and the baby.
4. Natalie smiled and said, "¡Qué chulo!"
5. The couple left their seats and went to Natalie.
6. The father explained about strangers and bad luck.
7. The father asked Natalie to touch the baby.

Vocabulary
2. Natalie was a stranger.
3. The parents were worried.
4. Praise from a stranger could make bad things happen to the baby.
5. The father held out the baby to Natalie.
6. Natalie held the baby.
7. Jon pointed to the parents and the baby.
8. Natalie could protect the baby by holding him.
9. Natalie had to touch the baby.

Dictionary Discoveries
(Answers will vary between dictionaries.)

UNIT 3

Comprehension A
2. F   4. T   6. F
3. T   5. F   7. T

Vocabulary
2. b   4. b   6. a   8. a
3. a   5. a   7. a

Dictionary Discoveries
2. no   4. no
3. yes   5. yes

UNIT 4

Comprehension A
2. T   4. T   6. F   8. T
3. F   5. F   7. F   9. T

Vocabulary
2. c   4. g   6. a
3. e   5. b   7. f

Dictionary Discoveries
2. /u/   4. /ʊ/
3. /u/   5. /u/

UNIT 5

Comprehension A
2. Arpi went to the United States.
3. Arpi started college.
4. Arpi met two Armenian sisters.
5. Arpi invited the sisters to her home.
6. The sisters arrived at Arpi's home.
7. Arpi served coffee.
8. The sisters left Arpi's home.
9. Arpi and the sisters explained their customs.
10. Arpi apologized.

Vocabulary
2. a   4. b   6. a   8. a
3. a   5. b   7. b   9. a

Dictionary Discoveries
(Answers will vary between dictionaries.)

Culture Capsule B
2. China   6. Italy
3. Germany   7. Japan
4. Germany   8. Mexico
5. Italy

UNIT 6

Comprehension A
2. T   4. F   6. T
3. T   5. F

Vocabulary
2. S   4. D   6. D   8. S
3. D   5. D   7. D

Dictionary Discoveries
1. V + N   4. V + N
2. V   5. V + N
3. N

UNIT 7

Comprehension A
2. J   4. S   6. J
3. S   5. S

Vocabulary
2. a   4. b   6. a   8. b
3. b   5. a   7. a   9. b

Dictionary Discoveries
2. stories   5. requests
3. days   6. women
4. themselves   7. movies

Expansion A

					[1]E	
[2]W	E	[3]D	D	I	N	G
R		A			V	
I		N			E	
T		C			L	
E		E		[4]B	O	O	K
R		R			P	
					E	

UNIT 8

Comprehension A

2. Jim put red pens on the table.
3. Some of the students didn't sign the forms.
4. Jim asked Ed to explain.
5. Ed explained the Korean Buddhist custom to Jim.
6. Jim put blue pens on the table.
7. The students signed the forms in blue.
8. The Korean Buddhist students got their money.

Vocabulary

2. b   4. a   6. a   8. b
3. b   5. b   7. b   9. a

Dictionary Discoveries

2. had   5. stood
3. gave   6. put
4. got   7. wrote

Culture Capsule B

1. T   3. F   5. T
2. F   4. T   6. T

Expansion A

```
Y  E  L  L  O  W
G  D  K  F  R  E
R  E  C  Z  A  T
E  R  A  O  N  I
E  U  L  B  G  H
N  C  B  K  E  W
```

(word search: YELLOW, GREEN, RED, BLACK, ORANGE, BLUE, WHITE)

UNIT 9

Comprehension A

2. T   4. F   6. F
3. T   5. F   7. T

Vocabulary

2. b   5. b   8. a
3. b   6. a   9. a
4. a   7. b   10. b

Dictionary Discoveries

2. arriving   5. getting
3. sharing   6. dying
4. hugging

Cultural Exchange B

2. f   4. e   6. g   8. d
3. h   5. a   7. b

Expansion B

2. kissed   5. greetings
3. hugged   6. briefcase
4. airport

UNIT 10

Comprehension A

2. Ted's grandparents jumped over the broom.
3. Ted and Mickey became friends.
4. Ted and Gail invited Mickey to their wedding.
5. The wedding began.
6. Ted and Gail were husband and wife.
7. Ted and Gail jumped over the broom.
8. Mickey looked surprised.
9. Ted laughed.

Vocabulary

2. h   4. d   6. c   8. b
3. i   5. a   7. g   9. f

Dictionary Discoveries

(Answers will vary between dictionaries.)

UNIT 11

Comprehension A

2. T   4. F   6. T   8. T
3. F   5. T   7. F

Vocabulary

2. S   4. S   6. D   8. S
3. D   5. S   7. D

Dictionary Discoveries

2. N   4. Y   6. Y
3. Y   5. Y

UNIT 12

Comprehension A

2. B   5. B   8. W   11. I
3. W   6. I   9. I
4. W   7. W   10. W

Vocabulary

2. e   4. g   6. b
3. d   5. c   7. a

Dictionary Discoveries

(Answers will vary between dictionaries.)

Cultural Exchange B

2. October 10, 1931 or 10/10/31
3. March 19, 1999 or 3/19/99
4. September 23, 2006 or 9/23/06
5. April 30, 2001 or 4/30/01

Expansion B

1. b   3. d   5. f
2. e   4. c   6. a

UNIT 13

Comprehension A

2. T   4. T   6. T
3. F   5. T

Vocabulary

2. Professor Singh followed the Sikh religion.
3. A Sikh's turban is a sign of pride.
4. The manager wanted Professor Singh to remove his turban.
5. Sikhs must wear their turbans indoors.
6. For Sikhs, not wearing a turban is disgraceful.

Dictionary Discoveries

(Answers will vary between dictionaries.)

2. a. /nɑt/; b. /nɑt/; same
3. a. /ɔf/; b. /əv/; different
4. a. /wɛr/; b. /wɛr/; same
5. a. /wɛr/; b. /wɚ/; different

Cultural Exchange A

2. f   4. a   6. c
3. b   5. d

Expansion B

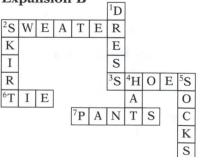

(crossword: 2. SWEATER, 6. TIE, 7. PANTS, 1. DRESSES, 3. SHOE, 4. HAT, 5. SOCKS, SKIRT)

UNIT 14

Comprehension A

2. Alfredo and Roberto wrote "Marino Vega" on their school forms.
3. Someone crossed out "Vega," and someone else crossed out "Marino."
4. The brothers had different last names for school.
5. The boys' parents went to the high school for Parents' Night.
6. Ms. Gillis met Roberto and Alfredo's parents.

Vocabulary

2. a	4. h	6. b	8. g
3. i	5. e	7. d	9. f

Dictionary Discoveries

(Answers will vary between dictionaries.)

Culture Capsule B

1. Wilson
2. Stevens, Cabot, Stevens-Cabot

Expansion A

Girls' Names
2. Barbara	5. Melanie
3. Abigail	6. Brianne
4. Daniela	

Boys' Names
2. Matthew	5. Brandon
3. Patrick	6. Charles
4. Nicholas	

UNIT 15

Comprehension A

2. F	4. F	6. T	8. F
3. T	5. T	7. T	9. F

Vocabulary

2. a	4. a	6. a	8. a
3. b	5. b	7. b	9. a

Dictionary Discoveries

3. ar/e/a   3
4. pros/per/i/ty   4
5. as/so/ci/ate   4
6. cre/ate   2
7. eight   1

Expansion A

NUMBERS CAN BE FUN.

UNIT 16

Comprehension A

2. T	4. F	6. F	8. F
3. T	5. T	7. F	

Vocabulary

2. a	4. a	6. a
3. a	5. b	7. a

Dictionary Discoveries

(Answers will vary between dictionaries.)

Expansion B

2. g	4. d	6. c	8. b
3. a	5. h	7. f	

UNIT 17

Comprehension A

2. F	4. T	6. F	8. T
3. T	5. F	7. F	

Vocabulary

2. D	4. S	6. D	8. D
3. S	5. S	7. S	

Dictionary Discoveries

(Answers will vary between dictionaries.)

Culture Capsule B

2. F	4. F	6. T
3. F	5. T	7. T

Expansion A

```
                              ¹S
      ²C                       T
      ³H A M ⁴B U R ⁵G E R      U
      I       O     I           D
      N       Y     ⁶O R A N G E
              L                 N
                                T
                      ⁷H A N D S
```

UNIT 18

Comprehension A

2. B	4. S	6. F
3. S	5. F	7. S

Vocabulary

2. d	5. h	8. b
3. a	6. c	9. f
4. j	7. e	10. i

Dictionary Discoveries

2. ex/per/i/ence   5. build/ing
3. in/side   6. in/vite
4. a/part/ment

Culture Capsule B

2. T	3. T	4. T

Expansion A

UNIT 19

Comprehension A

2. T	4. F	6. F	8. F
3. T	5. F	7. F	

Vocabulary

2. e	4. a	6. d	8. f
3. i	5. g	7. c	9. b

Dictionary Discoveries

(Answers will vary between dictionaries.)

UNIT 20

Comprehension A

2. T	4. F	6. F	8. F
3. T	5. F	7. F	

Vocabulary

2. a	4. b	6. a	8. b
3. a	5. b	7. a	9. a

Dictionary Discoveries

(Answers will vary between dictionaries.)